Preaching Deconstruction

Robert M. Price

Mindvendor
Raleigh, North Carolina

Copyright © 2014 Robert M. Price

Published by Mindvendor Books

Cover art by Carol Price after cover design of
The Gospel of Christian Atheism, 1967

All rights reserved.

ISBN: 0615953093
ISBN-13: 978-0615953090

Dedicated to
Bob Jackson,
friend, omniscient film historian,
and one of the most theologically
well-read people
I have met.

CONTENTS

Foreword	vii
Introduction	1
Derrida and Deconstruction	3
Saint John's Apothecary	14
Kettle Logic	25
Mask Without Face	38
Purloined Kingdom	46
The Place in the Text	57
Christ and Nihilism II	67
The Moebius Strip	77
The Fall of God	88
The Holiness of Desolation	96
The Fracture in Scripture	106
Mute Oracles	117
Jesus in a Bottle	128
About the Author	137

FOREWORD

Nothing in the Bible has so defied critical interpretation as have the parables of Jesus, parables that there is good reason to believe were unique to Jesus, and that were his primary way of teaching. Of course, this means that we know little about Jesus as a teacher, and yet he can be understood to be the most powerful teacher in history, at least to judge by his impact. Perhaps the greatest mystery in Christianity is Jesus himself, for despite the overwhelming attention given to him, he remains truly unknown to us, as though he is actually a mystery god, or a figure of absolute mystery.

Now Jesus was also an eschatological enactor of the Kingdom of God, but there is a fundamental problem in relating this to Jesus as parabler, although many understand his parables as parables of the Kingdom of God. Few are aware of it, but there is no actual writing of "kingdom of God" until the New Testament, and it is now clear that this usage of the "kingdom" is not to be confused with the reign of God as enacted in the Pentateuch. Jesus does not proclaim a reign of God, nor a kingdom in the literal sense, but far rather a new aeon or new creation, although some understand this as a primordial but wholly forgotten realm. Apocalypticism was extraordinarily powerful at the time of Jesus, as witness the Dead Sea Scrolls, and a controversial issue is whether the Kingdom that Jesus proclaims and enacts is an apocalyptic kingdom.

Robert M. Price

Jesus does enact the Kingdom of God, and this is his primary praxis, a praxis over which there is an immense controversy in Christianity, just as there is an equal controversy over the meaning of the parables. There is certainly no hope of resolving these controversies, but there is hope that these nonetheless can be enlightening, and if we do understand the parables as parables of the Kingdom of God, this can be a way of understanding Jesus himself. For Jesus does not only proclaim the Kingdom of God, he actually enacts it, and, yes, enacts it in the parables, which are not only parables in the common sense, but vehicles of transfiguration, and even of an absolute transfiguration.

Here, the first becomes last, even as the last becomes first, poverty rather than being lamented becomes exalted, as an absolute reversal occurs in the praxis of Jesus. Jesus is a revolutionary, but not a revolutionary in any established sense of that word, and nothing is a deeper mystery in Jesus than his identity as a revolutionary. Jesus was not a Zealot, not a political revolutionary, but rather a total revolutionary, or a revolutionary in every domain and sphere. This is what is most difficult to understand, and at this point no one is comparable to Jesus, just as none of our ideas or images of Jesus can here be effective.

Perhaps our most revolutionary envisioner of Jesus is William Blake, who finally knows Jesus as the "Self-Annihilation of God," as most decisively enacted in his final epics, *Milton* and *Jerusalem*. These are epics enacting a cosmic history, and a cosmic history of absolute fall and absolute transfiguration, which in a fundamental sense are centered in Jesus, and in the "Self-Annihilation" of Jesus. Blake was a

Preaching Deconstruction

great parabler himself; his parables are most clearly recorded in *The Everlasting Gospel*, and if only all too indirectly they play a genuine role in his final epics. Here, a cosmic reversal occurs, but one which is simultaneously a universal historical reversal, as everything whatsoever is absolutely reversed. Blake knows this reversal as most actually occurring in Jesus, who is the "Universal Humanity Divine," and the reversal occurs both in his praxis and in his crucifixion, and here praxis and crucifixion are inseparable.

The mature Blake is radically distant from the early Blake, yet only the early Blake is widely known, the Blake of "Songs of Innocence and Experience," which is vastly distant from the final epics. More than any other visionary, Blake created his own mythology as well as his own system, and here the primary deity is Urizen, who is finally realized as Satan. This occurs in *Milton*, and occurs through our most total vision of Satan, a Satan who is now realized as the "Self-Annihilation of God," a self-annihilation that is realized in Jesus. Blake was the first to enact the death of God, which occurs in his first prophetic poem, *America* (1793), but this enactment is not fully realized until his final epics. Then the "Self-Annihilation of God" is an absolute transfiguration of all and everything, but it is made possible by Jesus, and by the "Self-Annihilation" of Jesus.

Can we understand the parables of Jesus as playing a decisive role in this? If we understand them through a Blakean "Self-Annihilation" that would be a way of understanding their cosmic ground, and thereby we could understand the parables as enactments of the Kingdom of God. This would close a gap in our understanding of Jesus, a

Robert M. Price

gap between Jesus the parabler and Jesus the enactor of the Kingdom of God, and also a gap between the apocalyptic Jesus and the parabolic Jesus. Moreover, if we employ Blake as a primary way into Jesus we will certainly center upon the revolutionary Jesus, a Jesus commonly lost in our established understandings of Jesus, which in this perspective can even be understood as reversals of Jesus. Certainly Blake's understanding of Jesus is deeply offensive, but was not Jesus himself deeply offensive, and far more offensive than the gospels are able to portray?

Robert M. Price is unique in employing a common language that engages in an in depth analysis, so his is a book on the parables of Jesus itself employing a parabolic language, and thereby he gives us our most decisive way into these parables. No doubt this book will offend many, an offense necessary to any genuine book on these parables, and it is notable that few studies of the parables actually employ an offensive language. A book on the parables employing a contemporary Deconstruction will inevitably be offensive, but the parables have long been understood to be deconstructive in the common sense, and Deconstruction only deepens this understanding. The parables of Jesus are the first prophetic language employing an absolutely common and prosaic language, and this is honored by Price's book in an actual renewal of this language, and there could scarcely be a more decisive achievement.

Thomas J. J. Altizer
November 18, 2013

Preaching Deconstruction

One can be an "anachronistic" contemporary of a past generation, or the one to come. To be faithful to those considered of my generation, to be the guardian of a common if diverse heritage, means two things: To adhere, in the face of everything, to certain shared disciplines, from Lacan to Althusser, and including Levinas, Foucault, Barthes, Deleuze, Blanchot, Lyotard, Sarah Kofman, etc.; and that is without naming so many thinkers, poets, philosophers, or psychoanalysts who are happily alive, and from whom I have also inherited, and undoubtedly from others abroad, in even greater number, and who, for all their distance, sometimes feel closer.

    Jacques Derrida - "I am at war with myself." in: *Le Monde*. Interview. August 19, 2004.

The period of deferral is shrinking ever faster. More and more, because most of the thinkers that I am associated with are dead, I have been labeled a "last survivor;" because I am, along with some others, the inheritor of so many things, good and awful alike: the final representative of a "generation," the Sixties generation in a word.

    Jacques Derrida - "I am at war with myself." in: *Le Monde*. Interview. August 19, 2004.

Introduction

If anyone has understood this sermon, I wish him well! If no one had come to listen, I should have had to preach it to the offering box. - Meister Eckhart

Near the end of both my New Testament doctoral studies and my pastorate, I plunged pretty deeply into the works of Don Cupitt and Jacques Derrida, and into Postmodernism and Deconstruction. I found myself undergoing an intellectual transformation. On the one hand, Deconstruction made new sense of the Death of God theology, popular in the 1960s but which I read in the 70s — and loved! On the other hand, I saw everything with a new set of eyes. Deconstruction was, and remains, exciting. What a privilege, in the intervening years, to have met my philosophical-theological heroes Cupitt, Derrida, and Thomas J.J. Altizer! Call me a fanboy, I don't mind. I recognize the status of these thinkers as world-historical figures and am deeply grateful to have had even the slightest contact with them. I owe them so very much.

Robert M. Price

In the declining months of my ill-fated pastorate (though the use of such a phrase seems to lend more gravity to a forgettable situation than it deserves), I had come to inject a good dose of Deconstruction into my weekly sermons, no doubt hastening my departure from the pulpit. It is no surprise that typical, earnest, well-meaning congregants (whom I'm afraid I cannot refrain from calling "pew potatoes") cannot be expected to take much interest in any sort of theological novelty. Nor can I blame these dear souls. Do I sound patronizing? Rather, I say it would be patronizing to assume they ought to join me in my intellectual hobbies.

But I do think it was worth writing and preaching these sermons. They drew forth from me insights that benefitted me if no one else. They helped me to better understand both Deconstruction and the texts and questions to which I applied it. I guess I aimed them at the wrong audience, but that doesn't mean there is no audience for them. I suspect you may enjoy these sermons of mine in the same way. I guess it could be considered "niche homiletics." Welcome to the niche.

Robert M. Price,

November 24, 2013

Derrida and Deconstruction

"Deconstruction" simply denotes the kind of analysis you do on a machine when you take it apart to see what makes it tick. It is not particularly destructive, though it does come from Heidegger's term *"Destruktion."* We owe it to French philosopher/critic Jacques Derrida. I propose to review some basic points, or as he might say, axiomatics, of his approach.

We have to begin with the factor or condition of *differance*. Derrida purposely spells it with an "a" where both French and English readers would expect to find an "e" because he is trying to convey something both active and passive, neither active nor passive, something like the Greek middle voice. It is the fact of becoming different, of being different, of deferring, of delaying or postponing.

Differance is the condition of things becoming different. It thus precedes any of the different things. But it is not itself one of the things. One can only use the word "it," for differance, as Derrida says (again borrowing from Heidegger) "under erasure," that is, withdrawing it as soon as you say it. Grammatically necessary but actually impossible. For *differance* has no ontological, no metaphysical status. There is no "it" to speak of, except to speak of.

"It" is not like some Hindu All out of which all things emerge. It is simply a primordial factor. The priority of this condition means that there is no metaphysical grounding, nor any center of meaning from which all things gain meaning by their relations to it. The belief in a rational principle at the heart of things (including texts) Derrida calls "logocentrism." And brands it a fallacy and a delusion.

Differance has everything to do with language. As Ferdinand de Saussure has shown, without realizing the full implications of it, all language is a differential system of signifiers that derive their meaning only in their relation to each other. Yes, eventually, they are supposed to point "upward" to actual objects and concepts ("signifieds"), but as for the meaning of each signifier, it is derived from the sheer fact of its difference from the adjacent signifiers.

An "apple" denotes what it does because it does not denote what its close relatives "pear," "orange," "tomato," etc., denote. Think of pieces of a jigsaw puzzle. Each in itself is completely arbitrary as to shape. Yet each has a shape that is necessary in order to make the big picture possible. And whence does it derive this shape? Why, from the surrounding pieces! Nowhere else! *Differance* is the enabling condition of meaning.

Saussure granted that there were things and concepts signified by these differentially derived signifiers, but he said the signification could never be more than imperfect because of the shifting reference of words, the necessarily

Preaching Deconstruction

inexact correspondence between general dictionary definitions and the specific items we apply them to, etc. This hiatus was an unbridgeable "barrier" in the final analysis.

Everything Saussure left intact as a signified, however, Derrida demoted to a signifier. That is, there was nothing signified that was not itself a signifier pointing to something else, since there is nothing the meaning of which does not derive from the difference between it and something else. In other words, nothing escapes the field of *differance*, nothing falls outside the field of signifiers. There is nothing on the far side of the barrier. There is nothing outside the text. There is no "transcendental signified." Including some supposed normative meaning, let's say the intent of the author.

On this last point, let me hasten to add that it's not as if we can't sometimes and to some extent recover the intended meaning of the author (e.g., of Derrida or Saussure); it's just that the text has a life of its own, and when we read a text, it is usually the text, not the author, we are interested in. But it goes deeper than that.

Classically, philosophers and linguists have denigrated writing as a poor substitute for oral speech since the latter seemed still connected to the speaker. By tone of voice, by hand gesture and facial expression, by the possibility of re-explanation, the speaker could (supposedly) ensure correct understanding of his words. Writing, by contrast, was a much more slippery business.

The writer could do his best to make his meaning clear, but who knew what the reader would bring to the text? What distorting presuppositions, what biases or intellectual limitations? A writing was immediately orphaned by its father, cruelly set adrift; it could not be helped. Authorial intent cannot be contained as well in textual form, which anyone is free to interpret as he will.

But authorial intent must fight on a second front as well. As Derrida points out, Saussure has shown that language is already, before we speak it, an unstable, vital force, uncontrollable. And when we speak, it is out of a linguistic fund whose peculiar riches we can scarcely control.

This is not only because of language's own wayward nature. It is also, as Freud showed, because of the essential linguisticality of the subconscious itself. What, after all, is implied by the utility of word association tests, dream interpretations based on puns, and the revelations of "Freudian" verbal slips (like the time I was discussing funeral customs with my future in-laws and said I wanted a "closed casket wedding"!)?

All these familiar phenomena make pretty clear that the unconscious is a thoroughly textual beast, and a strange country in which no conscious intentionality of ours has ever set foot.

What this means is that when you write a text, you are really more like a mediumistic scribe merely holding the pen. Sure you had certain ideas in mind, but if you're like me, to a great degree, it will seem even to you that you simply *received* them. This is the more so the more fluently we write, the more it "flows." What we write flows out of the subconscious (the Muse), past the sluicegate of the conscious mind, coming from the dark wells below.

Preaching Deconstruction

The authorial intent is a mere epiphenomenon. What passes through the conscious mind of the writer as she writes is but the reading of the text by the conscious mind. And a different reader may well have a different reading. Something else may leap out of the text for a different reader, just as two people might see different things revealed in the same Rorschach inkblot test.

But let us be clear: it is the text, not its author, that we are analyzing. This is why the question, which seems increasingly silly to me, of whether or not the author might have had so and so reading in mind is utterly out of place. Again, think of Freudian slips in everyday speech. We can pretty well discern what a person intended to tell us, but the verbal slip tells us much more, and it is really contained in the statement, just as much as the intended meaning.

Since speech is just as much a creature of language, *differance*, and of a textual subconscious, the ancients were wrong: speech really can claim no advantage over writing. The speaker's subsequent "clarifications" are simply his own reinterpretations.

Much of Deconstructive criticism employs a Nietzschean play of words, etymologies, and puns. Derrida, like De Man, following Nietzsche at this point, always keeps in mind that all language is figural. All supposed metaphysics is really metaphorics. Just look at the spatial terminology on any page of Hegel, or the theological language trying not to lapse into myth that nonetheless speaks of God being "high and lifted up."

We have used words to death and have forgotten their metaphorical origins. When you call something "marvelous" do you really mean it is a miracle? Because that is what you are saying. When you say you suppressed your instincts, exactly where did you press them down? As a conscientious feminist, you might eschew the word "man" for "person," but you must have forgotten that "per-son" meant firstborn male child, thus heir. Uh-oh.

Some of the wordplay can be accounted for right here. If all speech is a palimpsest (a many times erased and written over sheet) of buried and forgotten meanings anyway, let's get to digging. Hence the etymologies.

Are you familiar with Heidegger? One of his most famous *Destruktionen* is that of the Greek word for truth, *aletheia*, in *Early Greek Thinking*. To break it down to its component parts, the word means "to take away the veil of forgetfulness," *a* being the negating prefix in "atheist," and *lethe* being "forgetfulness" as in the mythic River Lethe, the water of oblivion in Hades.

Heidegger knew that this derivation was no longer consciously in the minds of most Greeks as they spoke the word, since they soon abstracted it. Yet the original meaning was still implicitly present, having aimed the use of the word in a particular direction. And once you realize exactly what it first meant, you see that the history of its usage is illumined in a new way, as if the forgotten meaning of the word had continued to do its work silently all along.

Another approach to the style of wordplay exegesis is to keep in mind the Freudian technique of word association as a key to the subconscious. It is as if there is written into every text a textual subconscious as the residue of the subconscious of the writer. Her rational intentionality processed some of its conscious and subconscious ingredients in a rationally amenable and logically discursive way, but there may have been other elements that left their mark in other ways.

The logical tool of conceptual analysis, which we usually use in criticism, is not the way to detect these other dimensions of meaning laid down along other trajectories. Not conceptual analysis, then, but *punc*eptual analysis (as Gregory Ulmer, in *Applied Grammatology*, calls it). Unwitting puns or pun-like word resemblances, whether between words present in the text or implied as the differentiating traces of the ones appearing there (remember the jigsaw puzzle pieces?) may tell us much "of locked dimensions... out of reach except for hidden keys" (H.P. Lovecraft).

Whereas in conceptual analysis we seek linkages between related signifieds (ideas or objects) along a linear trajectory of a cumulative argument or exposition, in punceptual analysis, we rather compare related signifiers, words with similar shapes, since as dream analysis shows, such puns and near-puns, implied substitutions, hold secret meanings waiting to be decoded along a different trajectory.

Linguists have shown that every individual has an unconscious pattern of the usage of certain vowels and consonants, no matter how many combinations of these components he may use to say what he wants to say. Derrida is able to show that a writer will embed in his text a chain of apparently conceptually unrelated words with common or similar-sounding prefixes, suffixes, or roots. If we momentarily set aside the logical or narrative linear sequence (much as Structuralist critics do in interpreting myths) and set out the sets of similar-sounding or similar-shaped word segments, a pattern will form that is not fortuitous.

Wordplay exegesis, then, is a different way of carving the pie. It is putting a different lens on the scope to be able to analyze different dimensions. A conventional telescope is not going to be of much help for determining the chemical composition of a star. For that you need a spectroscope.

Poetry has several axes running in different directions, doesn't it? Rhyme and meter really have nothing to do with the story told in a poem, yet they are just as important. Neither can be neglected. Punceptual analysis is another way of tracing out such axes. This is quite appropriate since, as Derrida notes in his interaction with Mallarme´ in "The Double Session" (in *Dissemination*), all writing insofar as it is mindful of style and rhetoric is no less poetic than poetry. Punceptuality is one way of reading the poetry of prose.

I think of those usually unobtrusive railroad tracks one sometimes sees running at odd angles across a highway. One hardly notices them. They represent an entirely different trajectory of passage over the complex text of the traffic grid. Not like a cross street with a traffic light which governs your street as well. "Not in the spaces we know, but between them," Lovecraft says.

One day I was amazed to find myself suddenly stuck in a traffic jam on Route 46 in Northern New Jersey, amazed because a train was crossing the highway! I had never actually seen it happen before, and I haven't seen it since. In fact I had up till then wondered if the tracks were defunct.

Preaching Deconstruction

How could their operation not cause a terrible chain of accidents? Well, it didn't. In that moment I saw a living example of the kind of deconstruction practiced by means of punceptual analysis. It tries to spot that "graft point" where for a moment the two different kinds of signification intersect, creating a verbal anomaly or aporia (irresolvable loop) that tells us to look beneath the surface.

Derrida makes fascinating observations upon the potent ambiguities of the Greek word *pharmakon*, in his essay "Plato's Pharmacy" (in *Dissemination*). Strangely, this word carries seemingly diametrically opposite meanings. It can mean poison or remedy for poison (as when we use snake venom as a cure for snakebite). It can mean assassin or apothecary (like the druggist who sells Romeo a vial of poison). And furthermore it is impossible to keep these meanings out of each other's way! Each is heavily colored by the trace of its defining "other." There is a basic undecideability to the word, and thus to any discourse which uses it.

This Derrida shows in a discussion of Plato's account, in the *Phaedrus*, of the myth of the invention of writing by the god Thoth. He presents it to the king of the gods as a *pharmakon* for human forgetfulness. It will serve as a remedy for our tendency to forget important information. Even if we forget, no harm will be done, since we can always consult the written record. But the king rejects writing because it is a *pharmakon* for memory: it will poison memory, since, having the crutch of written records, people will rely less and less on their powers of memory and so lose them! And both are right!

Robert M. Price

It is not simply that the word has two different meanings and oddities occur when we use the wrong one (as when an acquaintance of mine once innocently remarked to British parents that their infant was "a cute little bugger," oblivious of the fact that "bugger" means "sodomite" in British parlance). No, *pharmakon* somehow means both at the same time. So for Plato to use the word, as he does in order to side with the king against writing in favor of speech, he introduces a computer virus into his program, a self-subverting counter-logic that causes his own text to war against itself, as we can surely see at least from the fact that Plato must present his argument in *written* form!

In such a case we have an instance of the phenomenon Derrida describes in his essay "Edmond Jabes and the Question of the Book" (in *Writing and Difference*). Verbal aporias like the *pharmakon* serve as a door into the text which is at the same time the mouth of a well, the gate into the bottomless abyss of language itself, the ever-turbulent pond of *differance* where every use of every word creates ripples in the field of signifiers, ripples that ceaselessly intersect as they endlessly rebound. And such is every text: an artificial framing of a given portion of the pond surface.

The deconstructive critic focuses now on this bit of the infinite text, now on that, as if to chart out a vast surface by triangulation, poring (pouring, aporia-ing) over the particular bits of wave pattern discernible in this portion, all the while knowing that it cannot be understood apart from what is beyond the margin of the piece he is studying. This is what it is because of the other that is what it is not. It receives its peaks and troughs because of a wave motion coming from somewhere beyond the area now under scrutiny.

All texts, all portions of the pond surface, are thus intertextual with each other, as Julia Kristeva dubs it, thus making possible the cross-fertilizing interpretation of one text by another. One understands each better insofar as one sees how close each spontaneously came (or can be read as having come) to the other, and how far away each stayed. Each is a Leibnizian monad-mirror in which the other may better be viewed.

Deconstruction rapidly becomes its own ever-weaving web of self-referential jargon, its own language game, not readily intelligible from outside the web, but quite illuminating from inside.

It is a whole new framework, and one does some things according to its rules that simply do not make sense in other frameworks. There is a limit to the amount of it that can be explained across the lines of the web. The paradigms, as Paul Feyerabend and Jean-Francois Lyotard remind us, are not finally commensurable.

Saint John's Apothecary:
Differance, Textuality,
And the Advent of Meaning

Anyone who has studied the Apocalypse of John, the Book of Revelation, may have deemed it odd that the book is ostensibly a revelation and yet it speaks in cryptical ciphers. It is the least understandable book in the biblical canon. What, pray tell, is revealed in it? Perhaps, as I will suggest, something about language and texts in general is revealed. Perhaps the Apocalypse precisely in the denseness of its code is the paradigm case of textuality. And this is disclosed through a deconstructive reading of the Apocalypse paralleling Derrida's exegesis of the *Phaedrus* in "Plato's Pharmacy."

John of Patmos did intend to reveal something, namely, the second advent of Christ, the soon coming of the end of the age, the final Parousia ("presence") of one called the Word of God. Why doesn't he say this plainly? All the strange figures of speech may have been a code to confuse the wrong readers should the book ever come into the hands of the authorities.

Another reason many readers have trouble making sense of the text is that they are simply not prepared to recognize what it is trying to tell us: that Christ will return soon, in the writer's own life time. That he didn't return is so obvious, so much taken for granted, like the very air we breathe, that the promise that he would come soon remains invisible. It simply doesn't occur to the pious reader that John might have meant that. And now that fact, the long delay of the Parousia of the Word of God, must be factored into any reading of the book, though originally, of course, it was not a factor at all. But it cannot be ignored. The delay must cast a new light on the text.

So the Apocalypse is a tissue of riddles and ciphers, promising an ultimate appearing of revelation, when we shall see face to face (1 Corinthians 13:12). I suggest that here we have in a nutshell an allegory of reading not only for the Bible in its entirety, but for all writing, all textuality whatsoever.

Every text is a page of code, of mute signifiers. This is clear to children who have not yet learned to read, or to adults looking at a page written in a language unknown to them. When we do learn to read the characters on the page, we are learning cryptography, how to crack the code before us. How to decipher the ciphers.

And all the while we are reading, decoding, deciphering, we are anticipating the meaning we will find, the truth promised us at the end of the process. We are waiting for the glorious appearing of some word of truth that will lighten our darkness and illumine our understanding. This is so whether you are reading the Upanishads or the instruction book for a new appliance.

But often that longing is disappointed, as full understanding does not dawn, as full recognition is delayed because either we cannot quite work out the cipher, or the language is open to many meanings, and we do not know where the truth lies. Text is cipher, and the promised Parousia of meaning always eludes us, makes us wait and wait.

Why does writing delay and defer and obstruct meaning? Jacques Derrida addresses these issues in a number of works including *Of Grammatology*. I want to focus, though, on his essay "Plato's Pharmacy" (in the collection *Dissemination*), where he deconstructs Plato's argument in his *Phaedrus* dialogue. There Plato, speaking through his ventriloquist dummy Socrates, tells a tale of the origin of writing. Here, in brief, it is.

Once upon a time, says Socrates, the messenger god Thoth came before the throne of his master Amon, king of gods and mortals. Thoth has a breakthrough, a great invention, to announce. His invention is writing. He says it will function as a *pharmakon*, a medicine, to make up for the infirm memory of human beings. If they write down what is important, they will not need to worry: should they later forget it, they can look it up.

But Amon is not so sure it is a good idea. This drug, this *pharmakon*, of writing, he replies, is not so much a medicine as it is a poison. It will but further erode the power of memory. People will take less care to remember precisely because they know they can always look up where they wrote it.

Worse yet, writing will steal the words from the author, wrest them from his control. A speaker may make himself understood, since he can repeat, rephrase, reinforce a point with a gesture or an inflection. A written transcription allows for none of these. Thus if I read a transcript of a speech I was not present to hear, I stand a much greater chance of misunderstanding it.

The speaker is the father of the word, and the spoken word is like the elder son in the Parable of the Prodigal: it stays close to home and obeys its father's behests, working under his watchful eye. The written word, the written text, on the other hand, is like the younger son who strays far from home, escaping the supervision of his father, that is, of its writer. With writing, there is more of a danger that meaning will get lost, will be harder to find, will be deferred. One may take longer finding the center of the maze. Worse yet, one may never get there and instead imagine that some *cul-de-sac* is the center! Derrida says that Plato is perfectly correct about writing. What Plato failed to realize, though, was that speech is no better! The same ambiguity he feared in writing already exists in speech, since it is inherent in language as such.

The kind of comparison Plato makes between writing and speech would really only make sense if he were instead comparing language on the one hand, whether written or spoken, and telepathy on the other. Only immediate, unmediated, awareness of the speaker's intent without the obscuring medium of language could prevent misunderstanding--or could it?

Do I even understand what I am saying? Really? Freud would have little difficulty in showing that I am at best a poor listener to my own internal speech, to the clues of my subconscious.

The problem with language is that it is a forest path with many winding branches, and it is easy to get lost. Thus the ciphers and puzzles of every written text, even those that on the surface seem easier to understand than the Book of Revelation. Language leadeth astray. At least it leads us a merry chase, the meaning an ever-receding will-o'-the-wisp.

Derrida noted that Plato had to employ writing even to make his complaint against it. And that even his apparently clear polemic against it is inevitably vitiated by the very ambiguity he seeks to exorcize. The best proof of the truth of Plato's complaint is the drift of meaning in his own essay, the fact, for instance, that the very same word *pharmakon* can mean both "poison" and "remedy."

A related word, *pharmakos*, can mean either "poisoner" or "scapegoat." And Derrida says Plato is making a scapegoat of writing, making it bear the curse of the ambiguity of language so that you will banish writing and then go on blithely relying on spoken language, forgetting that it is heir to the same infirmities.

Certainly he does not mean to admit this, but the words he uses speak for themselves. They are there to be read and for us to decipher, whatever he may have meant by them. The text speaks for itself. No *author*ity, not even the author, can be allowed to control the meaning of the text.

Preaching Deconstruction

Such is the nature of a text.

I am startled to find some of the very same moves being made in the text of the Apocalypse. John, like Plato, means to denigrate writing--even though to do it he must write! He means to exalt speech, the living Word of God who appears at the climax to banish the forces of textual chaos.

"Then I saw heaven opened, and behold! A white horse! He who sat upon it is called Faithful and True, and in righteousness he judges and makes war... and he has a name inscribed which no one knows but himself... and the name by which he is called is the Word of God... From his mouth issues a sharp sword with which to smite the nations, and he will rule them with a rod of iron; he will tread the wine press of the fury of the wrath of God the Almighty" (19:11-15).

When the Living Word appears at the finale, it is as if he has come as the spoken word incarnate to banish the evil of written textuality itself. He appears in order to defeat and bring to an end the very Book in which he appears!

John pretends that his Apocalypse is simply a transcription of what certain heavenly voices said to him, or what he saw with his own eyes. In other words, his text, he wants us to believe, is the thinnest of tissues. His unveiling (which is what "revelation" means) is itself a veil, but a transparent one--he says, or rather writes.

But he gives away the game with all his literary allusions to Daniel, Ezekiel, and Zechariah. It is obvious his text is a composite literary hash heavily dependent on earlier prophetic books, and by no means simply a showing forth of "heaven and its wonders and hell." It is a written text from first to last. Even if it is based on dreams or hallucinations he actually experienced, they have arisen from his subconscious clothed in the rags of remembered scripture texts.

It is the living, i.e., the *spoken* word that appears to wreak judgment, and yet his designation as the Word is "inscribed." Inscription is inescapable as the linguistic matrix from which speech proceeds, the matrix of meaning from which it emerges.

In the first three chapters he has the Son of God dictate letters to the churches of Asia Minor, and he pretends merely to take dictation. Yet even this spoken word, if such it be, is beset with ambiguity. Each letter ends with the appeal, "Let him who has an ear hear what the Spirit says to the churches." They end just like the equivocal parables of Jesus. In other words, they are ciphers essentially no different from the apocalyptic symbols later in the book. Are spoken words of God so clear? Remember the equivocal utterances of the oracle of Delphi!

At the very end of the book he warns in the sternest terms that no reader must venture to produce his own expurgated or interpolated edition of the Apocalypse: "I warn everyone who hears the words of the prophecy of this book: if anyone adds to them, God will add to him the plagues described in this book, and if anyone takes away from the words of the book of this prophecy, God will take away his share in the tree of life and in the holy city, which are described in this book" (22:18-19).

This is what regularly happened to these books of visions--take a look at Mark 13 and see what has been made of it in Luke 21 and Matthew 24! This is what John wanted to avoid. Don't take anything away from the book!

John knows that once he sets his pen aside and sends copies of the book to the seven churches of Asia Minor he cannot control what will be made of it. He cannot be sure what people will take him to have meant. If only he might have seen what Hal Lindsey and Charles Manson have made of it!

He intends that the prophetic word, frozen for transit into written text, will upon arrival melt again into living speech, since it is to be read aloud (cf. "the one who hears the prophecy of this book"), but he cannot even be sure people will not rewrite it in the meantime. So he strives to forestall the inevitable by means of this warning. Hands off, or it's the burning lake for you! He fears the latent potency of the *pharmakon*, the potent drug of writing, of textuality, of language.

And, again like Plato, he cannot decide whether the *pharmakon* is a poison or a remedy! Strikingly, the very thing he warns the would-be bowdlerizer not to do in chapter 22 he himself had done in chapter 10: "And when the seven thunders had sounded, I was about to write, but I heard a voice from heaven saying, 'Seal up what the seven thunders have said, and do not write it down'."

In other words, he thought better of a particular prophecy and struck it out of the final copy. That's textuality for you! John had become a hostile reader of his own text and censored it. What is a poison in chapter 22 had previously been a remedy, fixing the text in chapter 10.

John expects the Parousia of the Word of God to happen soon. But for now he must grudgingly rely upon codes, as in chapter 13 when he "tells" or thinks he tells the identity of the Great Beast with the cipher 666. Again, if he had only suspected the mischief this piece of text would cause!

There have been a thousand guesses as to who was intended by that particular cipher. And yet we need not look beyond the number itself. The written numeral 666 is not a reference to the Antichrist; by definition it *is* the Antichrist! If the Christ is the living word, that is, the spoken word, then the Antichrist is the opposite of the spoken word, namely the written sign *per se*.

So then, John grudgingly admits he is, we are, dependent on written signs now, but soon, he promises, true meaning will no more be impeded, detoured, delayed, re-routed by textuality. The New Jerusalem will descend and there will be no temple in it, as there was in the earthly Jerusalem. And why not? Because the old temple was a token, a reminder, of God's presence in his absence. But at the end of the world, the end of the *word*, there will be no need for reminders: God will simply *be there*, his Presence immediately dwelling amid human beings. Hence no temple.

And hence, also, no *writing*. It is in this same context that John drives out of the New Jerusalem a ragged crew of undesirables including the *pharmakoi*. "Outside are the dogs and *pharmakoi* and fornicators and murderers and idolaters, and everyone who loves deeds of falsehood" (22:15).

Who are the *pharmakoi*? Virtually without exception, Bible translations render the word "sorcerers,"

Preaching Deconstruction

but, remember, it also means "poisoners" and "scapegoats." (No doubt the word has all these meanings because, in ancient cities, when plague broke out, they would seize the local apothecary, already a dubious character who sold medicines, magic potions, and poisons, like the druggist in *Romeo and Juliet*, and drive him from the town, blaming him for the sickness and hoping thus to dispel it. "*Now* let's see you poison our wells!")

And remember Plato's *Phaedrus* with its Egyptian myth of the origin of writing. It is Thoth who invents writing. Thoth is a sorcerer and the dispenser of the medicine or poison of writing, a *pharmakos* in both senses. Just as Plato would have banished the poets from his ideal Republic, John is driving the dangerous magic of *writing* from the New Jerusalem as one drives a *pharmakos* or scapegoat from the city. He might have sent speech packing, too, since the two are accomplices in mischief.

But he is right: as long as God is not fully Present, any sacred writing or speech about God is but a token both of God's presence and of his absence. It is *present*, such as it is, but it is not *God*. It holds the place of the absent God. The Bible is a book mark, a book that is a mark, a sign for God, not the real thing.

Thus the written text of the Bible and the mute charade of speaking of the unspeakable God are medicine: they are a fix to get the reader by without the Living Water of the divine Presence. And yet that medicine is in the same moment a poison, the poison of idolatry. John drives the *pharmakoi* from the heavenly city arm in arm with the idolaters. The poison of the Bible's language is that it tempts the reader to make the stammering speech about God *into* God. The word "God" on the biblical page is the God that comes to be worshipped.

The text which pretends to reveal, whether that of the Revelation of Saint John or any other, is itself a veil. It is like the veil that hung before the Holy of Holies in Herod's Temple: it hides the fact that the Inner Sanctum is an empty chamber. The curtain allows the illusion that some Transcendental Signified awaits within. But in fact the veil itself is all that occupies the Holy of Holies. The text itself is the only thing revealed. It is a fabulous vista painted on a veil, not a transparent veil through which one sees a distant panorama.

Kettle Logic

Old Testament Reading: Isaiah 29:13-14

And the Lord said:
"Because this people draw near with their mouth
and honor me with their lips,
while their hearts are far from me,
and their fear of me is a commandment of men learned by rote;
therefore, behold, I will again
do marvelous things with this people,
wonderful and marvelous;
and the wisdom of their wise men shall perish,
and the discernment of their discerning men shall be hid."

New Testament Reading:
Romans 14:1-14

As for the man who is weak in faith, welcome him, but not for disputes over opinions. One believes he may eat anything, while the weak man eats only vegetables. Let not him who eats despise him who abstains, and let not him who abstains pass judgment on him who eats; for God has welcomed him. Who are you to pass judgment on the servant of another? It is before his own master that he stands or falls. And he will be upheld, for the Master is able to make him stand. One man esteems one day as better than another, while another man esteems all days alike. Let everyone be fully convinced in his own mind. He who observes the day, observes it in honor of the Lord. He also who eats, eats in honor of the Lord, since he gives thanks to God; while he who abstains, abstains in honor of the Lord and gives thanks to God. None of us lives to himself, and none of us dies to himself. If we live, we live to the Lord, and if we die, we die to the Lord; so then, whether we live or whether we die, we are the Lord's. For to this end Christ died and lived again, that he might be Lord both of the dead and of the living. Why do you pass judgment on your brother? Or you, why do you despise your brother? For we shall all stand before the judgment seat of God; for it is written, "As I live, says the Lord, every knee shall bow to me, and every tongue shall give praise to God." So each of us shall give account of himself to God. Then let us no more pass judgment on one another, but rather decide never to put a stumbling block or hindrance in the way of a brother. I know and am persuaded in the Lord Jesus that nothing is unclean in itself; but it is unclean for anyone who thinks it unclean.

TEXT:
Mark 7:1-13

Now when the Pharisees gathered together to him, with some of the scribes, who had come from Jerusalem, they saw that some of his disciples ate with hands defiled, that is, unwashed. (For the Pharisees, and all the Jews, do not eat unless they

Preaching Deconstruction

wash their hands, observing the tradition of the elders; and when they come from the market place, they do not eat unless they purify themselves; and there are many other traditions which they observe, the washing of cups and pots and vessels of bronze.)
And the Pharisees and the scribes asked him, "Why do your disciples not live according to the tradition of the elders, but eat with hands defiled?"
And he said to them, "Well did Isaiah prophesy of you hypocrites, as it is written,

'This people honors me with their lips,
but their heart is far from me;
in vain do they worship me,
teaching as doctrines the precepts of men.'

You leave the commandment of God, and hold fast the tradition of men."
And he said to them, "You have a fine way of rejecting the commandment of God, in order to keep your tradition! For Moses said, 'Honor your father and your mother'; and, 'He who speaks evil of father or mother, let him surely die'; but you say, 'If a man tells his father or his mother, 'What you would have gained from me is Corban' (that is, given to God) — then you no longer permit him to do anything for his father or mother, thus making void the word of God through your tradition which you hand on. And many such things you do."

I am afraid that after last week's sermon more than a few of you may have been left asking Rey Redington's favorite theological question: "So what?" That is, I argued that we can discern in the Apocalypse of John the lineaments of a polemic against writing on behalf of speech. This is not the agenda one would expect to find in a biblical book, which one might think instead to be taken up with more spiritual matters, issues closer to the axis of morality and religion, perhaps to religious authority. And what has the debate between writing and speech to do with *that*?

Much in every way, as Paul might say. In this morning's sermon I want to illustrate the crucial moral and spiritual relevance of the attempt to privilege speech over writing. And this time the object of my scrutiny will be Mark chapter seven, which represents the other side of the debate.

As Bob Jackson used to say about the wonderful films he screened here, this text moves on many levels. The surface level is one on which we see Jesus debating the scribes. They cannot understand why he throws to the winds the traditional practices of the Pharisee sect, in this case washing your hands before you eat.

Jesus is shown acting according to the maxim, "The best defense is a good offense," for he does not address their question for a single second. Instead *he* charges *them* with a more serious offense than flouting tradition. He says that they are such zealots for tradition that they prefer it to the Word of God. How so? While the commandment of the Torah bids us care for our parents, tradition declares one exempt from this duty if one's money be used instead for a religious donation. And, Jesus says, such evasions are all too typical of the scribes, who are hypocritical phonies pure and simple.

Yet is it unreasonable that a law might have its

exceptions on this or that point? The Gospels do not generally seem to think so. After all, Jesus himself is shown pointedly telling people to abandon their parents even on their deathbed and to preach the kingdom of God instead! If this isn't the pot calling the kettle black, I don't know what is!

For that matter, how can Jesus rebuke the scribes for inflexibility when it comes to healing on the Sabbath and yet be so absolutistic as the gospels make him on the issue of divorce?

It seems to me that the gospel writers are not interested in opposing the principle of fidelity to the biblical text to that of scribal interpretation, an opposition I am going to return to on my own terms in a moment.

No, the opposition they set up is simply between the voice of the scribes on the one hand and the voice of Jesus on the other hand. It matters not whether Jesus is consistent in his pronouncements. As they portray him, clearly he is not. It matters only that he said it.

The authority here is not that of an authoritative text. No, the text is batted back and forth like a volleyball between two would-be authoritative *voices*. Are you going to listen to Jesus or to those scribes?

But now let's go one level deeper. When we do, we see that the scene does not after all represent a confrontation between Jesus and the Jewish scribes of the first century AD. Several anachronisms make this plain.

First, it seems unlikely that the scribes would be so indignant at Jesus not practicing uniquely Pharisaic customs. These scribes were members of a pietistic sect. They knew quite well that the practices of other Jews did not coincide with theirs, nor did they expect them to. They would only chide Jesus had he been a Pharisee and neglected the practices, but then the whole point is rather that he doesn't even *mean* to follow them. He teaches another practice altogether.

And, as Bultmann says, the note that it is the practice of the *disciples*, not Jesus himself, that comes in for criticism, implies that the story arose in the early church. It is the practice of the Christian community, not that of Jesus, that is under discussion. Jesus is simply being invoked after the fact, as a fictitious precedent. As if he had had the foresight to solve the problem before it arose--in which case it would presumably never have arisen in the first place!

The debate is really one among two Christian parties, much as we see in Romans 14, where ritualistic Christians perhaps with a Pharisaic background, are pressuring their "stronger brethren" to adopt strict ritual practices. Mark's story is the propaganda of Gentile Christians, Paul's parishioners, who had no intention of submitting to the alien yoke of Torah observance. Note how Mark describes the scribal rules as the quaint customs of an exotic people, the standard view Gentiles had of Jews: "they do plenty of other things of the same kind, ritually washing cups and kettles and vessels of bronze. Imagine."

And it is a dead giveaway that the story has Jesus quoting from the Septuagint, the Greek translation of the Old Testament: "teaching as doctrines the precepts of men." The Hebrew, which is certainly what Jesus would have quoted to Jewish scribes (!), has "their fear of me is a commandment of men learned by rote," a rather different matter, I'd say. And the Hebrew wouldn't have made the point needed by the writer: man-made doctrines.

A Gentile polemicist quotes *his* Bible, the Greek Bible, to settle the question, attributing his exegesis anachronistically to Aramaic-speaking Rabbi Jesus. Jesus' holy name is a reinforcement in case the biblical argument should not be enough. Never mind the fact that the two warrants cancel each other out: if you've got the pronouncement of Jesus, it would hardly seem to matter much *what* the Bible says.

But it is *not* Jesus who speaks, and that is theologically important. It is a reader of the Bible, appealing to the written text and denying that the overbearing voice of tradition is the final authority. Writing here defends itself as a religious authority over against the imperious claims of speech.

Let me pause to tell you a bit more about the oral tradition that is the villain in this passage. Here is a crucial passage from the Mishnah tractate *Aboth*, or the *Sayings of the Fathers*: "Moses received the Law from Sinai and committed it to Joshua, and Joshua to the elders, and the elders to the Prophets; and the Prophets committed it to the men of the Great Synagogue. They said three things: Be deliberate in judgment, raise up many disciples, and make a fence around the Law" (1:1).

This was the warrant for the scribes of Jesus' day and for a couple of centuries afterward to compile a huge corpus of orally transmitted commentary and legal opinion on the fine points of the Law. Even with 613 commandments in the written Torah, many things were left unsaid. New situations arose and had to be prescribed for.

General principles set forth in the text had to be applied creatively to specific cases. For example, if a scorpion happened to scamper across the floor on the Sabbath, could you grab a kettle that lay ready to hand and trap it? No, because that would constitute *hunting*, a category of "work" which you couldn't do on the Sabbath! So said the scribes, in the name of Moses.

Their fiction of authority was that they were simply passing on the *rest* of what Moses had learned on Sinai but had not written down. Supposedly it was all said there on the mountain top. They were just repeating it. Or at least unpacking it. And their interpretations had the same binding force as the original.

Not all Jews accepted this claim. The Sadducees, for example, rejected the whole body of scribal tradition and insisted on remaining silent where the text was silent.

See how the two sides are drawn up, and over what issue: is a written text the authority, so that we ourselves might read it and come to our own conclusions? Or must we bow to the judgments of a class of experts who alone know what the text means?

A commanding voice seeks to control you, but a text will not speak to you at all until *you* give it voice by interpreting it to mean this or that. And precisely what it means is up to your judgment. When you read a text, *you* are the authority and must take responsibility, whereas when you yield to the commands of a speaking voice, to some guru or expert, you abdicate responsibility, you let someone else be in authority over you.

The same clash occurs in our Markan text. The writer is rejecting the supposedly authoritative voice of traditional interpretation, which had survived into Jewish Christianity, in favor of a written text, that of the Prophet Isaiah in this case. His own reading of it supersedes whatever the voice of the scribes may say.

Let's move forward some centuries to the time of the Protestant Reformation. Let's compare the theories of religious authority held by Catholics and Protestants. Both believed in an inspired, infallible, and authoritative book. Roman Catholics realized, however, that an infallible book didn't mean a thing as long as that book was ambiguous. The infallible truth may be in there somewhere, but it's hard to find, so if you want infallible guidance from it, what are you going to need? An infallible interpreter, of course! Thus the role of the Pope and the Teaching Magisterium.

How were Protestants to evade this logic? Their whole reason for rejecting Papal authority was the manifest fallibility of the Pope and his cohorts. How were Protestants to preserve the Bible as an infallible authority and, more importantly, as adequate by itself? Their answer was the doctrine of the "perspicuity of scripture." In other words, the scriptures are not ambiguous, at least where it counts. Any sane and reasonably intelligent reader ought to be able to see what it means and does not mean.

But this claim was and remains a hollow one. It was immediately refuted by the amazing proliferation of Protestant sects who of course all read the same text differently. And they lost no love for one another. Calvin had Unitarian Michael Servetus burnt at the stake.

And here is something dangerous about the doctrine of the supposed clarity or perspicuity of scripture. If you believe in it then you cannot afford to believe that there is genuine room to differ. You cannot afford to admit there are grey areas. So how must you regard those who differ with you? They must be heretics, schismatics, willfully blinded by Satan, or acting from self-serving motives, or even insane. Those who are so sure the truth is clear have little patience or tolerance for those who see the truth differently.

So what happened? The Reformers took their stand squarely for the written text as opposed to the voice of whoever happens to be sitting on the chair of Peter at the moment. But they could not live with the implications. They formed their own magisterium, wrote their own creeds. And those who dared believe that the text meant something different than Pope Martin *said*? You know.

Their problem was that they wanted a univocal and infallible teaching, a law to proceed from between the covers of the Bible as it once did from Sinai. A law governing belief and practice. Something we could all agree on and could be censured for dissenting from. And that a written text simply cannot give.

Why not? It is because of the essentially ambiguous nature of the written sign. This is what I said last week. Meaning in texts is always deferred, re-routed, detoured; never easily discernible, never unmistakable. Most definitely not something we can all easily agree on. Attend any Bible study and you'll see my point.

Look at the history of Bible interpretation, and you

Preaching Deconstruction

will see two things clearly: first, the Bible is a bottomless well of truth and transformation. When the inquisitive reader seeks encounter with it he or she is not disappointed. Deep speaketh unto deep. Second, there is little to no agreement on what the text means in any given case.

I know it seems that at least the members of a single denomination have reached agreement. This is why denominations have always debated so fiercely: each is sure that it is plain that scripture means what *they* take it to mean. But how do you suppose they reached the blissful state of unanimity that enabled them thus to close ranks against those differently convinced?

Of course, what happened was just that all the members of each denomination read the text, when they read it at all, through the interpretation of their pastors and official teachers. It was the spoken voice, not the written text that guided them. In the last analysis, all the Protestants had done was to play the Catholic game. They hadn't invented a new sport as they thought they had done. They had merely set up the American League alongside the National League.

I am maintaining this morning that we must invent a new game. One where one no longer wins by getting agreement. One no longer scores points by producing supposedly infallible and irresistible truth or commands from the Bible.

The Bible can be only the peculiar sort of authority a written text can be: one that raises questions, one that brings truth out of the being of the one who reads it, and the truth may not be the same for any two readers.

The authority of the text will be to catch us up short

with questions, options, perspectives we had not thought of. It will challenge us, make a bid for our agreement, but not simply reduce the mind or the will to dumb acquiescence.

We will find ourselves sent out by the risen Christ, not with a party line to which we must convert the nations, but rather like searchers in a scavenger hunt, chasers after meaning in the winding lanes of the world that is the Bible. It is a great huge world of many ideas and obstacles, not so different from the world outside the Bible.

You and I are fellow travelers in that maze. It will do us no good to complain that it is not a straight and direct highway with a clearly marked destination. Is that what you want? Would that be better? Would it be better if there were no mystery to life? If there were nothing left undiscovered?

The other week I had a long conversation with a young man fiercely committed to the notion of the Bible as an infallible guide book. I argued that God has granted us no such book, for all that we might wish that he had. He asked me why God would not have done so. My answer was to quote Lessing. He said that if God himself confronted him, offering truth in the one hand and the *search* for truth in the other, Lessing would unhesitatingly choose the search. Why? Because only the *search* for truth is suited to mortals. The *possession* of the truth is only for God. Only he could survive the Promethean consequences of having it.

And if you doubt that, look again at the deeds of those who are sure they possess the truth and that others who lack it must be evil and benighted. You will see a long and sorry epic of Inquisitions, pogroms, forced baptisms, Crusades, Jihads, heresy trials, jailings, beatings, and burnings. A history of bigotry and barbarism.

The search for truth exercises and trains the human spirit; the delusive conviction that one possesses the truth stunts that growth since it seems to render it superfluous. The possession of truth then becomes what the legend of Faust insightfully made it: a bargain not with God but with the devil.

Mask Without Face

Old Testament Reading: Psalm 33:1-9

*Rejoice in the LORD, O you righteous!
Praise befits the upright.
Praise the LORD with the lyre,
make melody to him with the harp of ten strings!
Sing to him a new song,
play skilfully on the strings, with loud shouts
for the word of the LORD is upright;
and all his work is done in faithfulness.
He loves righteousness and justice;
the earth is full of the steadfast love of the LORD.
By the word of the LORD the heavens were made,
and all their host by the breath of his mouth.
He gathered the waters of the sea as in a bottle;
he put the deeps in storehouses.
Let all the earth fear the LORD,
let all the inhabitants of the world stand in awe of him!
For he spoke, and it came to be;
he commanded, and it stood forth.*

Preaching Deconstruction

New Testament Reading:

John 16:12-15
I have yet many things to say to you, but you cannot bear them now. When the Spirit of truth comes, he will guide you into all the truth; for he will not speak on his own authority, but whatever he hears he will speak, and he will declare to you the things that are to come. He will glorify me, for he will take what is mine and declare it to you. All that the Father has is mine; therefore I said that he will take what is mine and declare it to you.

Epigrams:

"How do you see your role?" a black student asks me.
"I don't have a role," I reply. "I'm tired of all roles. I simply want to be myself. I don't want to wear a mask. I only want a face."
--Malcolm Boyd, Are You Running with me, Jesus?

"You once said that you were always changing masks, so that finally you didn't know who you were. I have only one mask. But it is branded into my flesh. If I try to tear it off--"
--Ingmar Bergman, Fanny and Alexander

Camilla: You sir, should unmask.
Stranger: Indeed?
Camilla: Indeed it's time. We all have laid aside disguise but you.
Stranger: I wear no mask.
Camilla: (Terrified, aside to Cassilda.) No mask? No mask!
-- Robert W. Chambers, The King in Yellow

Robert M. Price

Today is Trinity Sunday. It is the day when the church gathers to commemorate, if not to understand, the doctrine of the Three Persons of the Godhead. This doctrine emerged gradually in the late second century and came to flower in the fourth. It is never stated as such in the Bible, much less explained there. I would like this morning to draw brief attention to the ideas of three early church theologians on the Trinity, and the relevance they may have for certain persons we know a bit better than the divine Persons of the Blessed Trinity, namely you and me.

Let me begin with St. Irenaeus, the Bishop of Lyon in Gaul, originally a Greek speaker from Asia Minor. He wrote about 180 AD. As with other early Christian thinkers on the Trinity, he was very reluctant to say anything about the Godhead that might imply there was more than one God. Jews had complained (and still do, along with Muslims) that Christians were not very successful, despite their best efforts, at being monotheists. Don't Christians worship three different Gods?

Irenaeus understood the Father as the only deity. The Son Irenaeus identified as the reason possessed by the divine person of the Father. The Spirit, on the other hand, was the wisdom of the same Person. Of course you cannot draw any hard and fast line between a person and his or her reason on the one hand and wisdom on the other.

Son and Spirit, Irenaeus thought, became differentiated for the first time during the "economy" of creation and salvation. When the Father created the world he did this through his word, or reason, and his wisdom. When the Father appeared to humanity, he did so in the form of the Son, Jesus Christ. When he came at Pentecost to indwell his people, he did so in the form of the Spirit.

So Irenaeus appears to say that the threefoldness of the Godhead was merely potential, possible, before the acting of God in creation and salvation. We only know the threefoldness of God as it is revealed in the actions, the divine economy. What God may or may not be in his inner essence, we poor mortals cannot know.

Here is a teasing paradox: Irenaeus seems to be saying that what is revealed does not exist as such until the moment of its revelation. Now this is exactly the opposite of what we should ordinarily expect! Doesn't the very notion of revelation imply that a thing is already there, only hidden? The unveiling of it should make us able to see what was, but was invisible to us previously.

But, no, implies the ancient Church Father, it is only in the moment of the revelation of the threefoldness that God becomes threefold.

This is what Derrida calls the strange logic of the supplement. That is, it first seems as if a thing is adequate and complete. Then the thing is "supplemented" by a surplus, something in excess of the original: icing on the cake. But in fact, Derrida explains, the new added factor turns out to have filled an unperceived lack in the original, which is thus revealed as having been rather different from what we thought it was. So to *supplement* is to *supplant*, to replace. Even so, in Irenaeus' speculation, when God reveals what he is, he becomes greater than he was. He is therefore not revealing what he is but becoming something else.

Tertullian, a Carthaginian theologian writing in Latin about 20 years after Irenaeus, described the threefoldness of God as three *personae*. Persona, of course, is the word that gives us our word "person." But originally persona meant the mask worn by a Greek stage actor depicting his character--like the symbols of comedy and tragedy we still use.

To speak of the three *personae* of the Godhead carried the implication that, as in Irenaeus, the threefoldness of God lay in what we see, not in the inner being of God. From this the step is a short one to saying that God is one but plays three roles. This became known as Modalism, and was condemned as a heresy.

But I think it may be quite a helpful view, once one makes one modification. The fathers debated whether God was one in his primordial divinity, or three. Modalism said God is really, interiorly one, but that he externally acts in three ways.

Orthodox Trinitarianism said that, no, even in his inner being, God harbors threefoldness. Not only, to use the language of scholastic theology, must we speak of the economic Trinity, but also of the immanent Trinity.

I am treading deep waters here, I know, but please bear with me a moment or two more. We cannot do justice to Trinity Sunday unless we try at least for a few moments to penetrate into the Deep Things of God, the Celestial Arcana.

There is a great problem, from my viewpoint, in speaking of the ultimate Godhead as the immanent Trinity. To speak thus implies that God in his true presence to himself, his immanence to himself, is threefold. And this cannot be. As Derrida would say: to import threeness into the heart of supposedly ultimate Presence, the supposedly self-evident and foundational truth of all things, is to discover even in the God-Presence what Derrida calls "internal spacing."

That is, a Godhead which is already threefold in its first moment, which gains its meaning from each divine Person differing from both others, is already a derivative composite being, the end result of a hidden process of relation. The result is that there is no ultimate or fundamental Ground of Being.

To take this back to Irenaeus, he whom you found so abstruse until I got to Derrida, what I am suggesting is that there is no inner presence of God to himself. There is no immanent essence. God is what he is only in the moment of revelation, not before.

There is no divine self prior to divine acts. No divine entity standing behind his revelation and somehow different from it.

Irenaeus, I have said, compared the Son and the Spirit to aspects of the human person, his or her own reason and wisdom. A couple of centuries later, St. Augustine of Hippo would use a similar analogy. For him the Trinity may be compared to the intra-human trinity of memory, understanding, and will. Augustine defended the use of such analogies on the grounds that if the triune God had made human beings in his own image, then each of us must be Trinitarian in some sense as he describes.

Good point! And I would like to suggest that what I

have speculated concerning God, that he exists only in his actions, only in his revelation, applies equally to us humans. I think the sociologists Peter Berger, Thomas Luckmann, and Erving Goffman would back me up here.

Berger and Luckmann (in their book *The Social Construction of Reality*) point out how you and I only firm up a stable identity in the process of social interaction. It is difficult to know yourself by introspection alone. Indeed that is probably impossible.

For one thing, certain traits and attitudes presuppose interaction. One's character is in many ways a matter of whether one treats others well, how one responds to the good or bad actions of others. I can only know how good a Christian you are if I see you blessing those who curse you, praying for those who despitefully use you. You cannot be a Christian, even a person, in a vacuum.

For another thing, I can only form a self-identity, an estimate of myself, if I can react to myself and observe myself as I can react to and observe you. How can I do this? Simply by observing myself act, hearing myself speak. I objectify myself insofar as I act or speak. And here is Irenaeus' paradox again: I have no self behind my actions. Instead of my actions and words revealing the real me, they actually constitute the real me in the moment of speech or action.

Haven't you often enough found yourself accommodating your moral standards to your most recent behavior? This is what you are doing when you rationalize actions you once felt guilty for: the result is that not only do you not feel guilty for having done it, this time; you will not

Preaching Deconstruction

feel guilty for doing it next time either! Your actions took the lead, and your convictions follow in tow.

Haven't you committed yourself to something, perhaps rashly, and then felt bound to follow through? You became what you said. Watch what you say! Think before you act or speak! For when you act or speak, when you reveal yourself, you are in that moment creating yourself.

Since social life is to a huge extent a set of prescribed ritual interactions and roles, for you to become a person in social interaction (the only way you can become a person) means that you must choose to perform certain roles. You cannot simply create a new way of being human. You express your individuality by your choices among various available roles.

For instance, Sam, our sexton, and Tony DeLorenzo, have both chosen to play the role of artist. The role of artist has certain concomitants, not all of them pleasant. Artists suffer much. They have to: it's part of the job description, of the role. And it's somehow comforting to remember that in the bad moments: "This is as it should be, it is part of the role I have chosen."

I have chosen several roles, those of husband and father, pastor, scholar, writer. And the things that delight me the most are the things that are typical to the roles, not something that might be unique in my exercise of them. I rejoice in playing the role as it has been prescribed for me.

The Purloined Kingdom

Riddle Me This

Many of the sayings of Jesus are riddles. Jesus seems to have known that any truth he might simply tell you would not do you as much good as some truth you might come to by your own efforts. In this he was like Socrates who sought to coax his hearers to produce the truth from within themselves. That's where it was, if they would only realize it. As Tillich said, our problem is not that we are strangers to the truth, and so must be introduced to the truth from without, by someone else. No, our problem is that we have somehow become estranged from some truth that we really know, deep down. So we need someone to jog our memory, to prompt us to put two and two together. And so Jesus lets fly one of his sayings, followed after a pause with an implicit "Get it?"

Thomas, saying 5 is one such saying. "Jesus said: 'Know what is in your sight, and what is hidden from you

Preaching Deconstruction

will be revealed to you. For there is nothing hidden which will not be manifest." The saying assumes we are curious about some great mystery. There is some blank we want very much to fill in, and so we look for a way to get the information. Where to find it? "Say, isn't Jesus Christ a heavenly revealer? Why not go ask him?" Jesus the answer man. But he will not be cast in such a role, no matter how much traditional Christian theology may wish to portray him so. Theologians approach him with questions, but he answers them with more questions. And so here.

He seems to be saying that the mystery is not what or where you think it is. In fact, something only seems to be mysterious to you because you are failing to grasp something obvious. If you can figure out A, then Z becomes B, it falls right into line. Your problem is that you think you understand the basics, but you don't. And that is why something else seems so complicated. It wouldn't if you'd got off on the right foot at step one.

Recently I had an inexplicable malfunction on my fax machine. The machine is built to send me a printout self-diagnosis, but it couldn't give me a clue. I felt the headache coming on. What on earth could be wrong? No doubt some glitch in the dilithium microsubprocessors that I could never find in a million years. And then I discovered that the phone jack had slipped out of the socket. That was it. We ignore the simple thing before our nose and go on a great quest, a wild goose chase.

The disciples are all set to go on a safari for the mysterious truth. And Jesus tells them, save your trouble. What you're looking for is right at your feet. Don't you see it? "Know what is in your sight, and what is hidden shall be revealed to you." Because it is what is in your sight that is hidden in the first place. Somehow you do not see it.

Poe and the Police

As I read this saying, I thought immediately of Poe's tale, "The Purloined Letter." Had Poe known the Gospel of Thomas, he might have used the fifth saying as an epigram, because it is a perfect summation of the premise of the story. Perhaps you know it. It is one of the three adventures of Poe's pre-Sherlockian Sherlock Holmes, C. Auguste Dupin.

One day the frustrated prefect of the Paris police knocks on Dupin's door and tells how he and his men have been searching for months for a stolen letter, all without success. It seems that the queen had received some sort of love letter from a secret admirer and had hastily stashed it on her desk when the king came in. While his majesty did not notice the letter, soon a conniving government minister entered and did readily recognize the letter and what it meant. He managed to pocket it in plain sight of the queen who however dared not say anything lest the king be alerted to her indiscretion. The minister kept the letter to blackmail the Queen into favoring his policies. The Queen set the police on the trail of the minister to retrieve the letter as discretely as possible. They have made nightly searches of the minister's apartment, but to no avail. Every imaginable hiding place has been scrutinized with utmost care, but nothing. Eventually Dupin saves the day, reasoning that the minister, a clever rogue of his acquaintance, would have anticipated the secret searches and outwitted the police by "hiding" the letter out in plain sight in a letter rack on the mantel. No one thought to look there!

This particular story has attracted a lot of critical attention. Jacques Lacan discusses it in his "Seminar on 'The Purloined Letter'." Then Jacques Derrida critiqued Lacan, in his own "The Purveyor of Truth." Finally, Barbara Johnson mediated their debate in her "The Frame of Reference: Poe, Lacan, Derrida." I won't try your patience with the whole agenda of the debate, but here is something significant I got out of it. All the critics agree that in Poe's story the stolen letter functions as a symbol for communication in general. Every message, whether oral or written, is like a letter sent from sender to receiver. And just as the Queen's letter was stolen, and finally stolen again from the thief, every communication of ours is liable to go astray, to miscommunicate our meaning. A caricature of our words may return to haunt us. Our words may come to the ears of others whom we did not intend to hear them, and what was meant innocently becomes problematic. Every communication of ours may be misconstrued, its meaning lost in echoes.

And even when deprived of any particular meaning, the mere fact of the letter, of the thing having been said, is powerful and continues to make waves, as when, long ago, in a famous incident, Alexander Haig was embarrassed and discredited after the near assassination of President Reagan. He said, "I'm in control here in the White House," but the media did not hear the last few words and leaped to the conclusion that Haig was power-mad and had leapfrogged the whole line of succession. By the time they realized they were wrong, the damage had been done. Meaning had strayed; Haig's letter had been purloined.

Dead Letter Office

Reading "The Purloined Letter," I could not help but think of another letter, the Second Epistle to the Thessalonians. This was the passage that came to mind: "Now concerning the coming of our Lord Jesus Christ, and our assembling to meet him, we beg you, brethren, not to be quickly shaken in mind or excited, either by spirit [i.e., by a prophecy] or by word [i.e., oracle], or by letter purporting to be from us, to the effect that the Day of the Lord has come" (2:1-2).

There are a few places in the Pauline corpus where he mentions some lost letter. This makes New Testament scholars drool: a lost letter by Paul! Or in this case perhaps an early pseudo-Pauline forgery! Scarcely less intriguing! What is this letter? What happened to it? If only we might see it! What a mystery! Except that the mystery might well dissolve if we noticed something right in front of us. For more than likely the "lost" letter is simply First Thessalonians!

It might be that First Thessalonians, which does seem to say that the coming of the Lord is immediately at hand, is a forgery which Second Thessalonians means to correct. Or maybe it is Second Thessalonians which is a forgery trying to undo the damage caused by First Thessalonians, which

Preaching Deconstruction

had catastrophically disappointed people with a premature expectation of the Second Coming. Or maybe both letters are genuine, but Paul had not meant to say the Second Coming was quite *that* imminent, and he regrets that his letter had been misread.

In the few verses after those we just read in the second chapter of 2 Thessalonians, Paul lists the signs of the oncoming end, just to show that, since some of them haven't transpired yet, the apocalypse can't be expected immediately. One of these is the rise of the "son of perdition, who opposes and exalts himself against every so-called god or object of worship, so that he takes his seat in the temple of God, pretending to be God."

This thumbnail portrait of the Antichrist was derived from the attempt (39-40 CE) of the Emperor Caligula to install a divine image of himself to be worshipped in the Jerusalem Temple. You may be interested to know what happened next. When this plan was announced, the Jews sent an embassy to Petronius, the Roman legate in Palestine. They threatened an agricultural strike, martyrdom if necessary. Petronius realized how high the stakes were, so he sent a letter to Caligula, asking him not to send the statue. Caligula received the letter, didn't like it, and promptly dispatched a letter ordering Petronius to kill himself. The letter went on its way, but while it was in transit, Caligula himself died. This news, too, was sent to Petronius. Which letter would reach him first? The order to commit suicide, which as a loyal Roman he would have obeyed? Or the letter that would nullify the order to kill himself?

Petronius owed his life to the fortuitous circumstance

that the news of Caligula's death arrived first! His life had been saved by the purloining, the prolonging of the delivery, of the first letter. So the meandering, the straying of meaning, may be saving grace. The unpredictable dissemination of meaning may be the chance mutation that allows survival.

In any case, First Thessalonians turns out to be the Purloined Epistle mentioned in Second Thessalonians. "Purloined," as Lacan points out, derives from the same root as "prolonged" and implies the letter has gone astray before finally reaching its intended destination. And this is what happens, or at least what can too easily happen, in all of our attempts to communicate. Paul had tried to communicate the hope of an early Coming of Christ, but that promise was delayed, prolonged, purloined, and so the letter in which he said it became a purloined letter.

Epistles Intercepted

Indeed, at this point it occurs to me that all of Paul's epistles are purloined letters (and so is the rest of the Bible). Why? Because you and I, and all Christians of the twenty-first century, are reading these documents which were addressed to the concerns of people long dead. They have somehow become misrouted in the meantime! Whenever somebody in the early church collected these letters of Paul from the churches he had originally sent them to, he rerouted the letters. Ever since then, we have been reading somebody else's mail.

And that's where hermeneutics, the whole science of

Preaching Deconstruction

Bible interpretation, comes in. We need rules, as if there could be any, for redirecting a writer's words written for others, as if they were addressed to us. It's a pretty tricky business, full of ambiguity. And yet worthwhile. For no one would deny that we can eavesdrop on Paul's letters to Rome and Thessalonica and Corinth and pick up some valuable pointers. But in the last analysis, that's what we're doing: reading somebody else's mail.

I think it is significant that Islamic theologians deny that a letter could properly be considered scripture, since a letter is a word from one human being to another, not a word of God to humanity. I appreciate their insight that any word from God that we overhear must be very oblique, and the lessons we draw from it must be very tenuous. We simply have no business citing these texts as the conclusion of an argument, as a theological trump card. Paul wasn't trying to referee the particular game we are playing in the twenty-first century. He was in the first-century arena. So we have to be charitable in our interpretations of the Bible. Since mine is no less an indirect inference than yours, I had better listen to yours as seriously as I want you to take mine. Since we are both siphoning off meaning unintended for us, we had better be careful about it and not accuse each other of purloining Paul's letters too quickly, because that sword cuts both ways.

Paul's meaning was derailed, misrouted insofar as the Thessalonians mistook his meaning. And his meaning was something about the coming of Christ, the advent of the kingdom of God. And the confusion comes from the fact that that kingdom itself has been purloined, prolonged in its appearing. Lost somewhere along the way. Twenty centuries later, still it is as far from realization as ever.

Kingdom of Godot

And this brings me, after a long process of rerouting, following back alleys through the text, digressions and side roads, to another text in Thomas, saying 113: "His disciples said to him: 'When will the kingdom come?' Jesus said: 'It will not come by expectation; they will not say: "See, here," or "See, there." But the kingdom of the Father is spread upon the earth and they do not see it.'" This one might almost be a commentary on the fifth saying, with which we began. The disciples are scanning the horizon for the distant appearance of the kingdom of God. It is a great mystery, or so they think. They ask Jesus for some clue to know when the kingdom will come. But Jesus says there is no mystery such as they seek to solve. The kingdom has in fact already appeared. It is right before their eyes if only they will open their eyes and see it. When will it come? Nonsense! It has always been here! When are you going to start recognizing it? That's the real question.

Another point made in the Lacan/Derrida/Johnson discussion of "The Purloined Letter" is that the stolen letter functions both as a signifier and as something signified. That is, as a written letter, it says something about a state of affairs, specifically an affair of state, namely that the queen is having an affair that will, if discovered, shake the stability of the state. The letter says something about something other than itself. So it signifies. But once the crafty government minister recognizes precisely what the letter signifies, and purloins it, the letter itself becomes significant, an object of inquiry. The police search madly for it because it has come to mean something in and of itself. It has become a powerful weapon. It is a signified thing in itself, whatever the text of the letter specifically says. The police are scouring the place for any sign of it.

And in just the same way, the disciples of Jesus regard the kingdom of God as something signified. They ask for the signs that will signal its approaching. That, they think, is the mystery. They, and the whole Christian church, have sought for the kingdom as fervently as the prefect of the Paris police sought for that letter in every mysterious place he could think of to look. But like the Parisian police, we have wasted our time.

What Jesus says, by contrast, is that the kingdom of the Father is not that to which signs point. It is not some final meaning to be revealed. What no one suspected was that the kingdom was itself a signifier. A sign pointing to something else. In fact, pointing to everything else! As the Upanishads say, *neti, neti*: not this, not that. The Ultimate is not any one particular thing, but everything. The kingdom is spread out all over the earth--and we do not see it! We can't see the forest for the trees. We see all the finite things, but not the infinite sum of them. Schleiermacher understood the Redeemer's God-consciousness right well: it is "a sense and taste for the Infinite."

The Buddhists grasped it, too. Where do you go to find Nirvana, the unknown world of peace and eternal bliss? Do you retreat from this world to find it, as if there were some other world to take refuge in? No, you just learn to recognize that this weary world is Nirvana, once you open your eyes, once you stop expecting the world to be something other than the kingdom of the Father. How else can Jesus say you will see his face in the face of the least of his brethren? How else is it possible to look at bread and wine on the communion table and suddenly see there the body and blood of Christ? "If you will know what is in your sight, then what is hidden from you will be revealed to you."

Have you ever heard the truism, which is nonetheless true despite being an "ism," that life will be negative if you approach it negatively, but positive if you approach it positively? The world will be for you the kingdom of God if you expect to see it that way. The suffering of yourself and of others will be revealed as the crucifixion of the Son of Man. The continuance of your heartbeat from one fragile moment to the next will be recognized as the merciful providence of God. The extra strength, the second wind in your moment of extremity will be seen as the grace of God. The afternoon of boredom will become an epiphany of easy grace and the blessed space of freedom. It is already as plain as a city set on a hill, a light that suffuses the whole earth. Thomas' Jesus bids us to blink away the blinding scales and to open our eyes to the second sight of Isaiah, who in one moment saw nothing but an empty temple and in the next beheld the flaming seraphs who sang: "Holy, holy, holy is the Lord of Hosts; the whole earth is full of his glory!"

The Place in the Text

Old Testament Reading: Ecclesiastes 12:11-12

The sayings of the wise are like goads, and like nails firmly fixed are the collected sayings which are given by one Shepherd. My son, beware of anything beyond these. Of making many books there is no end, and much study is a weariness of the flesh.

New Testament Reading:

652.3Luke 4:16-21
And he came to Nazareth, where he had been brought up; and he went to the synagogue, as his custom was, on the Sabbath day. And he stood up to read; and there was given to him the book of the prophet Isaiah. He opened the book and found the place where it was written,

The Spirit of the Lord is upon me,
because he has anointed me to preach good news to the poor.
He has sent me to proclaim release to the captives
and recovering of sight to the blind,
to set at liberty those who are oppressed,
to proclaim the acceptable year of the Lord.

Robert M. Price

And he closed the book, and gave it back to the attendant, and sat down; and the eyes of all in the synagogue were fixed on him. And he began to say to them, "Today this scripture has been fulfilled in your hearing."

TEXT:

John 21:25
But there are also many other things which Jesus did; were every one of them to be written, I suppose that the world itself could not contain the books that would be written.

Last Sunday night I was talking to Tony DeLorenzo who mentioned a story by Borges called "The Library of Babel." In it we read of a reclusive order of scholars inhabiting a vast repository of books, indeed containing, if possible, every book ever printed. Thus ensconced, these imaginary archivists feel no need at all to exit their athenaeum to visit the outside world. Nay, what they have indoors is *better* than the outside world. It is the distillation and the analysis, the *essence* of the outside world, a knowledge of it better than the knowledge it has of itself.

The scene is similar to one in a film called *Slacker* in which we visit the adytum of a video-addict who shuns any light but that of the Cathode ray tube. He has flickering screens gazing at him from every point in the room, like neon bricks, between them the black mortar of stacked videocassettes. For him video is more real, in a Platonic sort of a way, than the world outside his cramped sanctuary.

Preaching Deconstruction

Once, on one of his rare trips outside the hive, he chanced to be walking past the entrance of a downtown saloon. Through the door sailed the limp form of a drunken man who lay across his path for a moment until another burst through the same door to knife the prone man in the back! Our video man had seen it all up close. And yet it was less real to him than something on TV, since he didn't have the image *on tape*. It would fade from his memory and could not be rewound and played back.

In both *Slacker* and "The Library of Babel" we have, I think, a satire on those who think they are so smart that they reveal their foolishness by letting life and the world go by while they remained fixated on some poor substitute for life. Isaac Asimov makes the same point in *Foundation* when he has a character rebuke a wealthy armchair archaeologist for remaining content with the rival theories of published scholars rather than going to the relevant site and doing some digging for himself.

Simon and Garfunkel sang, "I have my books and my poetry to protect me." To that these writers reply, "Get a life!"

This is a satire, I realize, aimed at *me*. You have seen my office. You have seen my home. You have noticed there an oddity of interior decoration: the wallpaper is not *parallel* to the wall but rather *perpendicular* to it. That is, the walls are practically everywhere lined and laden with books.

I am content to let much of the outside world go by. I am more interested in knowing what authors of texts ancient and modern have said, ancient scribes and modern theoreticians. My motto is that of the Beatles' Nowhere Man:

"*Ad hoc, ad loc,* and *quid pro quo.* So little time, so much to know!"

Have I and have the monastic custodians of Borges' Library of Babel taken up residence in the false imitation-world of books and escaped the real world outside the stacks? This morning I want to follow up a remark I made in last week's sermon about the Bible being a wide world in itself. I think I can show that in a crucial sense the situation is precisely the opposite of that described by Borges. The book is not a microcosm of the world; the world is rather a microcosm of the book, or at least contained within it.

Here again is the closing of the gospel of John: "There are also many other things which Jesus did; were every one of them to be written, I suppose that the world itself could not contain the books that would be written." In a book so filled with metaphor ("I am the door, the bread of life, the resurrection.") here is a surprising case of simple hyperbole linked to an unprecedented use of the first-person singular. Neither is Johannine idiom.

In fact the whole of chapter 21 of the gospel is surely an appendix. Note that the book had already concluded in the last verse of chapter 20: "Now Jesus did many other signs in the presence of the disciples, which are not written in this book; but these are written that you may believe that Jesus is the Christ, the Son of God, and that believing, you may have life in his name."

But some early editor decided to append chapter 21 with its rationalizing explanation of the embarrassing death of the last disciple, he who should have survived to the Second Coming but did not. And once he is done, he adds a

Preaching Deconstruction

paraphrase of the original conclusion. The point seems to be, "What you have just read is already one more of those Jesus-events the original author left out, and you might want me to add still more, but then that is a process that might never end. Where would one stop? Might as well stop now. We wouldn't want to flood the world with books."

Yet precisely such a scenario is envisioned in the Book of Isaiah when the prophet sees a future age in which "the earth shall be full of the knowledge of Jehovah as the waters cover the sea" (11:9b). The world will come to be contained within the book, within the text of divine revelation.

In fact it is *already* contained within the text. Roland Barthes (I find myself quoting him more often than *Karl Barth* these days) has said "All is text." Derrida has said "There is nothing outside the text," by which he means simply that we never view the world, we never see a single bit of reality, apart from some context of meaning. There is no perception apart from interpretation.

We are socially and religiously and culturally coached in advance as to what we see will mean. Reality is pre-inscribed as soon as you open your eyes. Zen Buddhists realize this. Their whole endeavor, as Don Cupitt has shown, consists in trying to abstract the world from the text in which it is pre-inscribed.

How ironic! Borges accuses the bibliomaniac of abstracting from the true reality of the outside world the shadow world of the book. And in fact the real futility would be to try and abstract a "real" world from the meaning-grids which alone allow it to make any sense to us!

It is obvious that a paper map is a tiny object within

the confines of the gigantic space of the world. Yet it is true that the world is contained within the text of the map. Insofar as our planet is an arena or theatre of meaning, of meaningful places, places to go for a particular reason, places to avoid, or to target, it is because the world has been contained in the text of the map. It has been supplemented with coordinates, points of interest, latitude and longitude, without which we are nowhere in particular. The world lies within the text, or it has no meaning.

That means, strictly speaking, that it is just impossible to be objective in our perception of the world. By definition we cannot look at it from any other perspective than that of an observer--otherwise we would not be looking at it at all!

And that is why one must devote oneself to a considerable amount of reading: the only way to broaden your perspective is to adopt different perspectives, at least on a trial basis. I can step out of my shoes, at least out of one of them, and put on yours and see things as you see them. But I cannot go entirely barefoot.

If I want to approach a God's eye-view, I cannot do the one thing necessary, to see with the all-seeing eye of God. I can only do the next best thing by adopting as many different slanted, biased, skewed and partial perspectives as I can. No one can view the text from outside the text, but we can assume different vantage points within the text--by reading books of different viewpoints.

And we have to do this for another reason as well. Ecclesiastes tells us that "of the making of books there is no end." That is, no particular book ever really comes to an end. There is no definitive boundary to any individual book.

Preaching Deconstruction

They all refer to each other even if only by implication.

When I read Borges's "The Library of Babel" I cannot help but seeing it as somehow linked to Thomas Ligotti's "The Library of Byzantium." I cannot help seeing the different points made by each story as being in dialogue, even though neither makes reference to the other.

When it comes to the Bible, the very phenomenon of the canon itself is a paramount case of intertextuality. Most of these books make no reference to one another. Many of them were written on the assumption that you would not be reading any others. And yet once you know the others exist it is quite impossible not to condition your reading of any one of them by the knowledge you have of the others. You cannot help reading Paul in the light of James and vice versa.

The world is contained within a text, and within a library of texts, which together form one super-text, a megatext. You cannot understand the world of your experience aright if you do not read that part of the world text, the world map of meaning that is the Bible. But equally, you cannot understand the world if the Bible is the only piece of the megatext you read. This is the problem of fanatics and zealots: they imagine that the text ends with the back cover of the one book they read.

What should you look for when you read the megatext of the book that envelopes the world? What part of the world are you trying to plot out as you read the map? Of course, you are primarily interested in the role of one particular character. A minor one, admittedly, yet not without interest: yourself.

James Fowler suggests that the much-asked question

of the meaning of life is really the question of just which *story* you are living out. Abstractions leave us cold. An idea, a formula, a concept is not the meaning of your life, and you know it. The meaning of your life is the *story* of your life, the story you are in fact living, whether a tragedy or a comedy, or perhaps *another* story you would *rather* live out, that you *dream* of living out.

The more you read, the more options, the more roles, the more possible stories there are to choose from. Are you looking to act the role of a starlet on a soap opera? Many young women are. Are you looking to repeat the story of Albert Schweitzer? I know some people who are doing that. I know people who have modeled their lives after that of Soren Kierkegaard, or of characters in a Bergman film. Some choose fairy tales, some choose tragedies, some epics.

And you can live the story out in your own way, to the extent circumstances allow you, on your own modest level. The great epics of antiquity may make the stories of our lives seem modest, even pitiful by comparison. Yet their grandeur is simply our small life-story written large so everyone can see. They are lines shouted by the actors on a stage so everyone in the theatre can hear. They are larger than life only in the sense of Platonic forms, prototypes.

Listen to the Lukan Jesus, proclaiming his messianic role in the Nazareth synagogue. He finds the place in the text where the career of the liberating Servant of Jehovah is set forth. He reads this text and reads himself into it. "Today this scripture is fulfilled in your hearing." What does this mean?

That centuries earlier some clairvoyant had

envisioned Jesus' own career and written it down in advance? Nonsense. What has happened is that Jesus reads a story in scripture, the story of one anointed with the Spirit of liberation, one who will spend his life setting the captives free, and he has decided that this is the story he will live. This, and no longer the splitting of boards and the selling of chairs, will be the meaning of life for him.

But you are not living the story of the Liberator. You are perhaps living the life of one of the oppressed, one of the captives who awaits the coming of liberation. What binds you? What is the nature of the prison you are in? I wonder if your life frustrates you because you are playing out a script for a role you are not by nature suited to play. You are stuck with a story your parents chose for you, or that society dictated, or that your fears have forced you to accept because you do not believe you are capable of a happy ending.

Does society tell you that you cannot choose this or that life story because of your color or your gender? All right. You cannot change that. That is bitter gall. But there is still a choice of stories. Will you play the contemptible victim who makes a phantom motion of re*sis*ting by merely re*sen*ting? Or will you craft another version of the tale? There are, you know, endless variations on a theme. Aren't there other ways of doing what you want to do or of utilizing your talents?

It may be that your new take on an old theme will prove to be better than the original. Shakespeare's *Hamlet* is a reworking of an already hackneyed theme, but it was such a work of genius that it altogether supplanted those earlier versions that it imitated.

What is the story you are born to live? What is the epic for you? Young Werther? Faust? Gilgamesh? Joan of Arc? Semiramis? Van Gogh? Mine, I will tell you, comes partly out of the biographies of Harnack and Baur, partly out of M.R. James. Maybe yours will be something nobler. I congratulate you. But whatever it is, read. Discover more of the options. Let no one else decide. And sit down and plan how you may live your story, even if you have to do it in your spare time.

The world exists in the text. The text is endless, encompassing all books. And somewhere in that limitless volume you will find your story. Your life is a place in the text which alone lends it meaning. Read and mark and let it be fulfilled in you.

Preaching Deconstruction

Christ and Nihilism II

I would like to share with you this evening what I perceive to be the hidden meaning of two passages of scripture which both use the image of light shining forth from darkness at the very moment of creation.

The first is the Priestly account of creation in Genesis One. In it we read that God uttered "Let there be light!" And the light, which did not yet exist, nonetheless did not deem that a sufficient excuse to delay obeying the Almighty voice.

The second is the introit of the Gospel of John in which all is created by the Word, the Logos, of God, and that Light was the light of reason, that which enlightens everyone who enters the world. In this latter text what we see is that the creative utterance of God in the Genesis passage has been filtered through the Stoicism of Philo and the Hellenistic Judaism of the day. The Word has become a semi-autonomous divine entity alongside God.

What is a word? It is to speak one's mind. The Word, or Logos, comes in Hellenistic philosophy to be nearly synonymous with the mind. It is God's mind, and it enlightens us as well. As St. Augustine would put it, we see all things by the light of the Divine Intelligence.

But both passages mention not only light but darkness as well. Darkness is the nearly tangible, obtuse bulwark against which the light flares forth in the dawn moment, when utter chaos gives way to the light of reason.

Behold, I show you a mystery: that darkness which light dispels is the very medium of light, for the light needs the darkness in which to shine. Without darkness to dispel, light would be invisible. It can only be seen for what it is in its difference from the darkness in which it shines.

Think of it like fire. If there were no air, there would be no fire. It cannot exist in a vacuum. Fire needs oxygen to burn. Even so, darkness is the oxygen of light. Light means nothing, and would be nothing, without its twin and opposite, darkness.

And in the same way, we must admit that darkness is logically prior to light. Darkness is there first, and then light bursts forth. Chaos is prior to order, randomness to meaning. "Thou whose almighty Word / Chaos and darkness heard / and took their flight." Chaos and darkness were already present when the Word first sounded.

Tillich put it this way. Being and Nonbeing are opposites. But of the two, Nonbeing is older, because in every moment, Being is an affirmation of itself over against Nonbeing, which hence must be prior to Being, at least logically, if not chronologically.

All this, it seems to me, is quite biblical. And yet we have never acknowledged the theological, ontological implications. But I think Jacques Derrida has appeared in a prophetic role, much like Nietzsche's mad prophet, to tell us the implications, like them or not.

Derrida calls attention to the "logocentric" nature of Western philosophy. This means that the light of reason is exalted over everything, and that there is a rational truth about all things, a "logos-structure" as Tillich calls it, which makes it possible for there to be an over-arching truth to understand, and for the human mind, eventually, to understand it.

There is a universal light of intelligibility to things, and it appears reflected like light in the mirror of the rational human mind. The task of philosophy, according to logocentrism, is simply to polish the mirror of the mind so that we may reflect the truth more clearly. So that we do not see in a glass quite so darkly. That is what philosophical and theological argument is for.

But Derrida brings the idol of logocentrism crashing down. First he points out that the Logos, a rational meaning, simply cannot be prior to the world it supposedly explains and underlies. Why? Because the very condition of the phenomenon of "meaning" at the same moment *undermines* meaning! How?

Think back to what I said a moment ago: light seems to be the opposite of darkness. The two words would seem to be as different from one another as two things could be, right? But light means nothing without darkness to shine in! It requires the presence of its opposite in order to be, to mean, anything at all!

This is true with every signifier, even with everything supposedly signified. All meaning is differential in character. It is like the binary language of computers. A is not non-A. But it is thus entirely dependent upon non-A for its meaning as A! A has meaning only as the opposite of non-A. We cannot say what either A or non-A is, except by reference to the other. Each is the defining, the originary trace of the other. Each is integral to the meaning of the other.

Every meaning implies its opposite. As Tillich always maintained, faith is the opposite of doubt, and yet it includes doubt, it does not banish it! If it did, it, too, would fade away. One word's differing from its neighbor, and only in this way attaining any meaning at all, means that there can never be any clear truth as opposed to error. To speak of a rational order is to say that something has been artificially ordered! To say that God is one, as does the Shema, undermines the unity of God, since the very notion of *oneness* demands a prior notion of *many* against which the assertion of oneness is made. One *of* many! One--*instead* of many. A narrowing down of many to one. An *exclusion* of other gods, not an absence of them.

Light, reason, order, meaning, then, are not ultimate. Right reason, the Logos of God, is the tip of the iceberg of madness.

To assert one overarching meaning is only made possible by the condition of meaning, namely *differance*. Unless meaning were an unstable arc of tension back and forth between opposites, there could be no meaning, and since this is so, ambiguity, randomness, difference are more ultimate, more fundamental.

If there is a light of the world, it can comprehend the

darkness no better than the darkness can comprehend it. And in fact it is the darkness of chaos which can be said to create light.

What of human reason? Does it reflect the light of truth? Does not truth seem self-evident to the mind? That was good enough for Descartes: what presents itself as clear and distinct to my mind must be true. But Derrida says this, too, is an illusion. The self-presence of the mind in the present moment, as David Hume saw long ago, is an optical illusion.

The present moment receives the apparent meaning and color it seems to have only by virtue of remembering the past and anticipating the future. By itself the present is empty, blind and naked. In the same moment we embrace the conclusion of an argument as clearly true, we have already begun to forget the steps that led us there. We have to go back over it in our minds to remind ourselves and be convinced again. And again.

Even our self as we appear to ourselves is largely a product of censoring and editing by the subconscious mind. Others can see what we cannot. Others know us better than we know ourselves. If we cannot see even the eye that sees, how sure are we that we are really seeing anything else?

Derrida was concerned to upheave the edifice of Western philosophy, which he has done to my satisfaction. He began with Plato, a devout servant of the rational Logos. Plato said that speech is always better than writing, even better than a written account of the same speech, because the speaker is the father of the Logos, of the word. (Does that phrase have a Christian echo to it?)

The speaker has a definite idea in mind and seeks to communicate it by word, helped along by voice, stress, gesture. He is present in his utterance, and if he speaks well, his intended meaning is present in his words as they enter the mind of the listener.

But the father of the word, when he commits his word to *paper*, is sending out a prodigal son which may not stick to the intended path. The text meets readers without benefit of the presence of its author. Readers must make of the text itself what they can, and they may get a totally different meaning out of it.

That is a built-in liability of a written text. It speaks for itself, no matter what you had in mind, and it may not say the same thing. The meaning of a written text is uncontrollable.

But Plato's condemnation of writing, to which even he had to resort, is too little too late. He is locking the barn door after the horse has got out and run away. Derrida's accomplishment is to point out that meaning itself, the whole system of language itself, is *already* a field of chaotic text even as it is written into your subconscious. You are always saying many unintended things every time you open your mouth. The word is immediately like a can of worms that cannot be got back into the can. The fatal ambiguity of writing has always already attached itself to speech, too--in fact, to all language as such.

The Bible implicitly recognizes this linguistic chaos when it says that for now "all is in parables," i.e., nothing is definitively clear, all is equivocal. The light of the world may shine on everyone who comes into the world, but it is evident that we are seeing it in a glass darkly.

The Christian claim, however, is that one day the truth, the clear light of the Logos, the meaning of the world intended by the Father of the Word who spoke it into ordered existence, will appear plainly. This will be the full presence of truth to the mirror of the intellect. It will be the Parousia, or "presence," of truth, and on that day we will "know even as we are known." Language will no more be misleading and ambiguous. Meaning will no more lie in the eye of the beholder. "I have said this to you in figures," the Logos of the Father says, but "the hour is coming when I shall no longer speak to you in figures but will tell you plainly of the Father." A glorious Parousia of authorial intent!

Is there such a single truth, a central sun of Logos, meaning, about which everything else revolves? That, alas, is the very error of logocentrism which Derrida has debunked, whose bluff this mad prophet has called. By the very nature of truth as a function of *differance*, there can be no one truth, no truth prior to error, no objective truth.

As Nietzsche said, as his madman screamed, God is dead! The earth has become unchained from the sun of meaning about which it once orbited, or *seemed* to orbit! The Logos-center has been shot out of the sky like a clay pigeon!

There is no truth independent of language, standing outside it or above it, no Transcendental Signified. There is no meaning outside that could be imposed onto this field of signifiers, this ocean of words, of text.

Reality is a word-search puzzle, an abstract painting, and the only meaning it may have is what you project onto it. That is what God did, after all. He decided that it would mean thus and so. *But that is only one opinion.* There is no central truth to the thing itself!

Reality is, paradoxically, full of meaning for you to find there, simply because it has no *one* meaning! If it did, it would be a cold, dead thing, a mere stone. But it can mean anything because there is no one definitive meaning at all! This is the Nihil, the crater. It is the Nothingness that is no thing, no-one-thing.

Some have quailed and become sick at the prospect that reality is an empty canvass, that there is no picture painted upon it. But, as Nietzsche knew, the knowledge of the Nihil is a joyous knowledge! Because you face the virgin canvas as God did on the morning of creation! A palette of paint is in your hand! The picture is for you to paint! The world of meaning is for you to create! Who else could do it?

The Nihil, the pulsating Void that is full of potential because it is nothing actual, is in some ways like the traditional idea of God. It has a kind of phantom ultimacy, precisely because it is no one penultimate thing. It bears the will-o'-the-wisp trace of holiness, a kind of echo of transcendence. We face the abyss of metaphysical nullity and exclaim, slack-jawed, "Why is there Nothing rather than Something?" And thus there is a kind of negative worship left unto us. A *Via Negativa*. The Logos is dead. That should be a familiar notion to us here on Holy Saturday.

But that is by no means the end of Christ. If we embrace the Nihil, we renounce forever the notion of Truth. We admit henceforth that all is fiction, and that is a gladsome realization! A cause to celebrate! From this point

Preaching Deconstruction

on, we say that all meaning is fiction. A meaning of our own creation. A story which provides meaning as we act it out. Does it correspond to ultimate reality? No, because nothing can: there is no ultimate reality.

Fiction is the only kind of truth there ever was. And we can adopt the fiction of the New Testament, the wondrous tale of a Messiah who set forth the conditions of discipleship and said "Follow me!" Did he do miracles? Did he even exist? Who knows!

But we understand the story, "the old, old story," and we know well enough what discipleship to this Christ entails. We can choose to live his story. We can choose that meaning for ourselves. If others choose another fiction to act out, fine: let them. We can only tell them they are welcome to join in our Mystery Play should they wish.

The Empty Tomb of Christ is the Void left by the absence of any central, objective meaning of things. That Christ, that Logos that is the Only Truth and the Only Way, is dead. In fact he is doubly dead, never having existed in the first place, retroactively dead. But Jesus died on the cross, and rose into the Gospels. The flesh was made word, and we dwell amongst it as we adopt for ourselves the fiction of Christ and Christianity.

Do you, then, stand upon the brink of the universal crater, facing the Nihil? Then you do what God did on the first day of creation. Speak and create!

Robert M. Price
Holy Saturday 1993

Robert M. Price

(The original "Christ and Nihilism" was an Easter sermon delivered by my pastor and predecessor at the First Baptist Church of Montclair, Donald Morris. This is an unauthorized sequel.)

The Moebius Strip

Jesus saw children who were being suckled. He said to his disciples, 'These children who are being suckled are like those who enter the kingdom.' They said to him, 'Shall we, then, being children, enter the kingdom?' Jesus said to them, 'When you make the two one, and when you make the inner as the outer, and the outer as the inner and the above as the below, and when you make the male and the female into a single one, so that the male be not male and the female not be female, when you make eyes in the place of an eye, and a hand in the place of a hand, and a foot in the place of a foot, and an image in the place of an image, then shall you enter the kingdom.' **Gospel of Thomas 22**

You have noticed, I'm sure, how our little service retains vestiges of a conventional church service, just as Christian services retained the bare outlines of the Jewish Synagogue service. One such vestige is a sermon, and specifically a sermon that attempts to explain and apply a passage of scripture. Like Schleiermacher, like Calvin and the Puritans,

I still see the role of the minister as that of a servant of the word. I feel the chill of reverence for the Holy Text, whether that of the Christian canon, of the heretics, of the other religions. And I feel most at home in the pulpit as a midwife, trying to bring to birth insight from these ancient texts. It is alchemy, the transformation of papyrus into wisdom, of superstition and myth into spirit and truth.

Again, it is agriculture, as I make to scatter the potent seeds of the ancient writings into your minds where it may take root, and all manner of exotic fruits may bloom. This morning's text is certainly one of the more exotic variety. Or you may think in terms of another metaphor. It is perhaps a stony field from which it seems nothing may grow. It is a blank wall with only gibberish scrawled on it. What is Jesus, or Judas Thomas, saying?

I believe the code has been cracked. Like the Book of Revelation, you just have to learn the code and it all clears up. At least I think it does, unless it is even more of a puzzle than it looks. And I guess it is. As Frank Kermode says, all texts are first and finally obscure, a dull obsidian in which we dimly discern meanings that are but our own reflections. Well, here goes nothing.

The passage before us comes from the context of early Christian baptism, specifically from the circles of Encratite Christianity. These were the Christians who made celibacy a condition of salvation, and who had many women prophets and teachers. They had renounced sexuality, seeing in it the downfall of Adam and Eve, and thus they had gone beyond sexuality and beyond chauvinism.

The image of the newborn baby suckling is a common

image for a new initiate into Christianity or the other Mediterranean Mystery cults. You are a catechumen who is fed the milk of introductory doctrine. Then you became one of the *telioi*, the mature, the perfect among whom Paul might preach secret wisdom. The children, then, are the newly baptized.

They have made the two one. How? It is really rather simple. To use Kierkegaard's phrase, they have attained unto that "purity of heart" that means "to will one thing." William James, in *The Varieties of Religious Experience*, says that the conversion experience has the effect of setting the religious sentiment at the center of the personality so that all other interests take their place in obedient orbit around it. There is a centrality of the spirit. The two, or more, have become one. As Jesus says elsewhere, you cannot fire two arrows at the same time. You cannot ride two horses in different directions at once. As James says, if you are double-minded, you will never achieve anything. You will be like the two-headed giant who always quarreled with itself, never able to agree on what to do or where to go. You must make the two one. You must get your self together!

You must "make the inner as the outer," so that the distinction between them is lost, like in the mysterious Moebius Strip which seems to have two sides, but each becomes, and thus already was, the other. This, too, though difficult in practice, is really a simple thing. You know all those places where Jesus criticizes people for being like whitewashed tombs: pure and unsullied outside but full of corruption inside? Where he says something's badly wrong if a fig tree bears grapes? The inside and the outside should be the same. You ought to be transparent. Everything should be on the surface.

Live in such a way that afterward there will be no nasty discoveries. Like the great literary critic Paul de Man. Most knew him as a conscientious and generous mentor and scholar. After his death, lucky for him, someone unearthed a bunch of Belgian wartime newspapers in which de Man had written articles friendly to Nazi anti-Semitism. They published the newspaper, so he would do what they said. He was a yellow Nazi stooge. Everybody was pretty upset when they found out. If de Man hadn't been dead already, this would have killed him! Don't be one thing outside and another inside.

"Make the above as the below." I admit this would fit better if it had "Make the below as the above," but maybe he means "close the gap" between God's will and your own, much like the petition in Matthew's prayer: "Thy will be done on earth as it is in heaven."

"Making the male as the female and the female as the male." This is likely a reference to the transcending of sex roles through the abjuring of sex. Genesis 2 had the man and the woman becoming one, but it was through sex, not through the renunciation of it. The Encratites seem to have believed that Christ was the second Adam in the sense that he restored the original androgynous character of humanity before the first human had been split into male and female. Thus he had gone back before the entry of sin. Baptism, as Galatians 3:23 says, identifies you with this Christ, the result being that there is no longer any division of race, class, or sex, any more than there was in the primordial human being

Preaching Deconstruction

before the division.

"Eyes in place of an eye": remember the admonition to rip out and cast away your offending eye? That probably refers to lust or coveting or stinginess. To replace such an eye would mean to replace these habits with an eye that is sound and full of light. To change your perspective on things.

"A hand in place of a hand": same thing. The Sermon on the Mount also says to cut off the offending hand and throw it as far away as you can. To cut off the hand, in Aramaic idiom, George Lamsa says, is to stop stealing. As 1 Thessalonians says, "Let him who stole steal no more but work with his hands."

"A foot in place of a foot": We are told to cut off the offending foot and throw it away lest it lead us into a worse fate for the whole person, final damnation. Lamsa says that to cut off the offending foot means to stop going where you should not go, a euphemism for adultery among other things. Not to trespass.

An image in place of an image? Thomas seems to hold the same sort of idea of the resurrection we find in 1 Corinthians 15. Now, as mortals, we bear the image of the earthly, the fleshly Adam. But on Resurrection Morning, we will bear the splendid image of the heavenly Adam, the Adam Kadmon, the heavenly prototype of humanity. Humanity as it was before the fall. Again, very much like Encratite Christianity, not to mention the Jewish Kabbalah.

So in all these cases, the newly converted is told to live a new life, turn over a new leaf, adopt new habits. If he does, he will attain unto the kingdom.

Robert M. Price

What I have just done is what Jonathan Culler and other critics call "naturalizing" the text. Every text stands before us like an alien hieroglyphic. Just as Ventris had to learn how to decipher the hitherto unknown Mycenean script Linear B, just as you must learn German to read a German text, and before you do, it looks like gibberish to you--every text is a hill that must be scaled with some effort. You may be able to leap over it and not even be winded. But it may take several tries. You may have to give up and skip it. A very dense text is like Mount Everest. Can anyone scale it? If you do, they will say you have "conquered" Everest.

When we make what we think is adequate sense of a thorny text like Thomas 22, we think we have conquered the text. The text was our opponent, like Jacob wrestling with the god of the River Jabbok. So we wrestle with it till the sun comes up, and if we are tenacious enough, saying to the text as Jacob did to his antagonist, "I will not let you go till you give me a blessing," we may indeed get some spiritual light from the text.

But have we found the meaning of the text? De Man would say what we have done is to rewrite a text we couldn't understand into a new, simpler text that we *can* understand. We have reduced it, whittled it down, domesticated it. Made it manageable. Just as we do when we evade the admonition of Jesus to love our enemy or to give to the poor, pretending it says something else, something less, something that we already agree with.

What we have done is to allegorize the text, just as the Stoics did with their scriptures, the Iliad and the Odyssey, when they recorded unedifying deeds of the gods. No, the

Preaching Deconstruction

Stoics reasoned, the texts must mean something else. The embarrassing gods must stand for something else, something we like. As when Genesis 1 plainly says the world was made in less than a week! We can't buy that, but we hate to say the Bible is wrong, so we say, in effect, "Let's pretend what it says is that God made the world in six vast aeons of indeterminate length." It would be nice had the text said that--but it didn't! Every interpretation, one critic has said, is an allegorization, a translation of one set of terms into another, more manageable. And Thomas speaks with some pretty strange sounding terms. Maybe we ought to leave them sounding strange and raw. Maybe the point is to let them act on us like baffling Zen koans.

Let me return to some few points in the saying, to look at them in a new light. A light that emerges when we do not smother the piercing light of the text under the bushel-basket of conventional, sensible meanings.

"When you make the inner as the outer, and the outer as the inner." Here I am reminded of an intriguing observation made by Raimundo Panikkar. He draws attention, in an almost Derridean way, to a contradiction in our spiritual imagery. We speak of internalizing the external, as when we speak of taking the eucharist. You are symbolizing the reception of divine grace as if it were a matter of taking the spirit from outside and drawing it inside. Billy Graham asks you to ask Christ into your heart. From the outside in. But, Panikkar says, what has come in has only changed exterior positions. As long as it is other than you, it is outside you. For it to be truly inside you, it must become the same as you, *homoousion*. The two must be made a single one. If you are to get God inside you, you must get God to *become* you!

The early Sufis, like the martyr mystic al-Hallaj, knew this. They were Muslims, members of that religion which will countenance no partners for God, no other Gods. But they reasoned to the conclusion that if anything but God even *exists*, then it is a rival to God. Therefore only God exists, and as Shankara said, we are the same as God. Al-Hallaj used to go about outraging the orthodox by saying "I am the Truth!" It is more humble, he taught, to say "I am God" than to say "I serve God," since the latter still allows a being beside God to usurp the divine prerogative of being!

"Make the above as the below." I said a moment ago that the interpretation I offered would work better if it said "Make the below as the above." But this time let's take it as it stands. Make the above as the below. Here I have little choice but to think of Altizer, the evangelist of the Death of God. The Sacred has been poured out into the Profane. God is present only as the Trace, the Shadow, the Echo, the Cinder. As the Kabbalah says, God has withdrawn to allow room for the world to be. But even the cosmic crater of God's absence is a mode of God's presence. The above has become nothing else than the below. Nirvana has been revealed as Samsara. All things glow with the ultraviolet brilliance of the absent God. In another text from Thomas the disciples ask Jesus when the kingdom will come. He says, "What you anticipate has arrived but you do not see it."

"Make the male and the female a single one, so there is no longer any male and female." Celibacy? Maybe, but I'm not interested in it. Suppose instead the idea is that the male adds female characteristics, while the female takes on male traits in addition to the original female.

This is what the Jungian June Singer calls Androgyny. You know that Jung hypothesized that every man has a hidden female counterpart inside, his *anima*. Likewise, every woman has a man inside, an *animus*. It is as if to say your unconscious self is the opposite gender. One is manifest, the other latent. One dominant, the other recessive. The same thing is reflected in physiology, isn't it? The man has secondary female characteristics like nipples, while the female has secondary male characteristics. Even the genitalia mirror one another, having diverged from the same basic model.

Or think of it like the Tao, divided by an S curve into two complementary opposites, Yin and Yang. They need each other. Their very identity, their shape, is determined by each's difference from the other. Each is the Trace of the other and nothing else. That is the way of male and female. And each has an anticipation, a latent bit of the other in it. In us it has to do with relative amounts of testosterone, the presence or absence of a Y chromosome. But every male has a bit of the female, every woman some of the essence of a man. It gives us enough commonality to be able to understand each other, though not enough so that we can understand each other without trying hard.

June Singer advises us to cultivate the counterpart within. As Deborah Tannen says, we need to learn each other's assumptions, desires, priorities, reactions. And we need to empathize, to think in the other's language and to speak it ourselves. If we do, we will be awakening our anima or animus. It will be a kind of psycho-sexual ambidextrousness--using both hands, both sides of the brain with equal facility. In fact, it won't just be *like* it, that's exactly what it will *be*.

This is quite real to me personally. I believe I have always had some feminine sensitivities. Once my mother told me that had I been a girl they had planned to name me "Lynne." From then on I felt that Lynne was the name of my anima, my female counterpart within.

I believe one reason Carol and I get along so well is that in her some of the latent male traits have come to the surface. She is a no-nonsense realist. She is at home in the real world as I am not. She is canny and shrewd, and has better judgment than me. She has an awakened animus just as I have an activated anima.

This is why she can be my lover and my best friend. She is male enough to be my buddy and female enough to attract and delight me. Let me venture a speculation on what happens with a good marriage. I dare say that the man gains the dimensions of his anima from his mother, his female role model, and we hope she is a good one, while the woman has her animus shaped by her male role model, her father. Men can thus say, "My mother, myself," and women can say, "My father, myself."

Then one meets a member of the opposite sex who answers to one's own inner counterpart. This is why we relate to the opposite sex in a similar way to the way we related to our opposite sex parent. Once one meets the right partner, and they grow together over the years, the spouse more and more becomes the mate's anima or animus. Each of us externalizes our counterpart, projecting it onto our mate, and the mate internalizes it. Carol replaces "Lynne" or becomes Lynne, my anima. We are one. The two have been made one.

And this, in turn, is how we come to have "eyes in place of an eye." Notice that in this phrase a single part is replaced by more than one. In a sense we have a reverse of the imagery of the rest of the text, where two are made one. Here one is replaced with two. Just as Hercules would lop off one head of the Hydra, only to see two more sprout in its place. When the counterpart is awakened, whether by your becoming one with a mate, or by cultivating your own inner double, you see yourself from a new perspective; you begin to see yourself as others see you. I often catch myself thinking, "Come off it, Price! That's just typical apish male stubbornness. You know better than that!" Thanks, Lynne. Thanks, Carol. I needed that.

But if you did this, if you awakened your inner counterpart, wouldn't you have in fact done the opposite of what the Gospel urges? Wouldn't you be making the one into two? No, I don't think you would. You are assuming you are already one. That's where you're wrong! As it stands now, you are a half! You are a Yin by itself, a lone Yang, a bicycle with one pedal. You're not going to make much progress that way. Let the half become whole. Let the two, one of which is now buried and hidden, join and become one. And then you will have entered the kingdom.

The Fall of God

Old Testament Reading:

Genesis 3:1-11, 22-24

Now the serpent was more subtle than any other wild creature which the LORD God had made. And the serpent said to the woman, "Has God said you shall not eat of any tree of the garden?" And the woman said to the serpent, "We may eat of the fruit of the trees of the garden; but God said, 'You shall not eat of the fruit of the tree that is in the midst of the garden, neither shall you touch it, lest you die.'" But the serpent said to the woman, "You will not die. For God knows that when you eat of it, your eyes will be opened, and you will be like God, knowing good and evil." So when the woman saw that the tree was good for food, and that it was a delight to the eyes, and that it was to be desired to make one wise, she took of its fruit and ate; and she gave some to her husband with her, and he ate. Then the eyes of both were opened, and they knew that they were naked; and they sewed fig leaves together. And they heard the sound of the LORD God walking in the garden in the cool of the day, and the man and his wife hid themselves from the presence of the LORD God among the trees of the garden. But the LORD God called to the man and said to him, "Where are you?" And he said, "I heard the sound of thee in the garden and I was afraid because I was naked, and I hid

Preaching Deconstruction

myself." He said, "Who told you that you were naked? Have you eaten of the tree of which I commanded you not to eat?" [...] Then the LORD God said, "Behold, the man has become like one of us, knowing good and evil; and now, lest he put forth his hand and take also of the tree of life, and eat, and live forever--." Therefore the LORD God sent him forth from the garden of Eden, to till the ground from which he was taken. He drove out the man; and at the east of the garden of Eden he placed the cherubim, and a flaming sword which turned every way, to guard the way to the tree of life.

New Testament Reading:

Luke 17:20-21
Being asked by the Pharisees when the kingdom of God was coming, he answered them, "The kingdom of God is not coming with signs to be observed; nor will they say, 'Lo, here it is!' or 'There!' for behold, the kingdom of God is in the midst of you.

Text:

Gospel of Thomas, saying 3:
Jesus said, 'If those who lead you say to you, "See, the kingdom is in heaven," then the birds of the air will precede you. If they say to you, "It is in the sea," then the fish will precede you. But the kingdom is within you. If you will know yourselves, then you will be known and you will know that you are the sons of the Living Father. But if you do not know yourselves, then you are in poverty and you are poverty.'

Last week we took the briefest possible look at the Eden story.

Robert M. Price

Today I want to return to it. Let's see if I can manage it – or whether I will be turned back by that cherub with his flaming sword!

Let me summarize for you two very different accounts of the separation of God and human beings. The first is that of Saint Augustine, followed by the whole of the Western Christian tradition. In this version we are to understand that God posed fledgling humanity a simple test: he arbitrarily chose one single tree and told the primal pair to keep their hands off. But they just couldn't resist the lure of forbidden fruit.

In this interpretation Augustine was perhaps unduly influenced by his own Tom Sawyer escapades in which as a youth he made away with pears from a neighbor's orchard. From this episode he learned the lesson that forbidden fruit is the sweetest.

In any case, humanity failed this simple test. As a result we inherited both the guilt and the taint of sin. God had no choice but to drive our first parents out of Eden, as his eyes were too pure to look upon sin. From there on in, our acceptance by God is a chancy matter, made possible only by extraordinary favor shown from on high.

But as Saint Augustine saw it, the distance had not even yet been overcome, since even after Jesus Christ, we *remained* sinners sold under the bondage of iniquity. Doomed forever to moral and spiritual defeat, yet forgivable thanks to Christ.

Here is the other account, in some ways the opposite of the first. It is the theory of the 19th Century Hegelian Ludwig Feuerbach. (Feuerbach's very name, by the way, is redolent of mythology: it means "the Brook of Fire," the Phlegethon!) He postulated a primordial shirking of human responsibility, a primeval repudiation of the divine image in which nature had cast humanity. So far it sounds rather like Augustine, doesn't it?

But according to Feuerbach, 'twas moral cowardice did the deed. We had divinity in ourselves, all the godly traits of

Preaching Deconstruction

righteousness, love, nobility, justice, faithfulness and the rest. In short, all the divine attributes were first ours. But we were too lazy or too self-distrustful, so what we did was to fantasize the existence of another being who could vicariously bear our righteousness.

We decided there was a divine being up there in the clouds who was perfectly loving, just, righteous, etc. To endow him with these perfections we had to empty ourselves of them. We had to bow and scrape, to confess our unworthiness and his entire worthiness. For him to be morally perfect, we had to call ourselves totally depraved. Theologically we said it would be presumptuous to claim for ourselves what was his alone. Namely, righteousness in all its forms.

"Only thou art holy!" So chants the worshipper, and it sounds pious, but Feuerbach says it is the greatest blasphemy against the spirit, the Holy Spirit of Man, who must be unholy if only God is holy.

Feuerbach knew he would be called an atheist, but he said he believed in the reality called God; he just wanted to put it back where it belonged: inside the human breast.

These accounts, those of Augustine and Feuerbach, at first seem to be antipodal, as opposite one another as two views could possibly be. Yet I suggest one could hold both at the same time. In fact, to me, they are merely the two sides of the one coin.

Both stories tell us that man and woman renounced their righteousness, their divine image. And both agree that as soon as this happened there sprang into being what had not existed before: a vast distance between man and God.

It was Thomas J.J. Altizer who first helped me see this (I paid him back one day, let me assure you! Once I helped him find the right subway to the San Francisco airport!).

Altizer somewhere theorizes that man is alienated from God because of the Fall. But equally and in the same moment,

Robert M. Price

God becomes transcendent of man because of this alienation. His ways are not our ways, he is high and lifted up. You must go seek him in his temple. Because he no more walks among us in the cool of the evening.

For man to be fallen away from God is for God to be *transcendent*. And for God to be transcendent is *the Fall of God*! Alienation was mutual. A fallen humanity means a transcendent deity, the alienation from man of the divinity innate in him but now banished by his own act! There would have been no other God separate from us but for the fall. So it was equally the fall of man and the fall of God.

But Jesus Christ came to negate the effects of the Fall, did he not? He has joined the separated. He has knit into one piece that which was sundered. In him the God has come near who once was afar off. His kingdom is close at hand.

And thus the answer of Jesus to the questions posed him in today's gospel readings. Where is the kingdom of God? It is not out there somewhere, as if one might go somewhere else to find it. As if one might spot it if only one took up a powerful enough telescope. No, the way to *miss* it is to look for it out there somewhere, because all along it has been right *here*!

If it is here, then the way to lose it is to go off somewhere in search of it. If I think I have misplaced my car keys, but in fact they are just where I thought I put them, then I am only assuring myself that I will not find them as soon as I start canvassing every place *else* where I think I might perhaps have lost them!

This actually happened to me a few years ago. I finally went to the trouble of replacing all my keys, only to find them many months later just where I thought they were in the first place!

And strangely enough, it is just as easy to forget where the keys of the kingdom are! And when you do, religion will be erected on a false premise. Life will become a quest throughout

Preaching Deconstruction

the universe and the heavenly spheres to find something that all along was near you, in your mouth and in your heart: the Kingdom of God.

You can see another example of the same dynamic in the same chapter of Luke we read from. The disciples said to him, "Lord increase our faith." They thought they lacked it because they were looking somewhere else for it, but their very words showed where it already was: within them. Their very request showed they had it! Or did they ask him for faith in a spirit of cynical hypocrisy, never for a moment entertaining the possibility that he might answer their prayer? They already had faith or they would never have asked the question to begin with!

What if...? Every time you bemoan your sinfulness, your lack of the moral perfections of God, all you are doing is reinforcing the false belief that you don't *have* them! You are a sinner all right --because you tell yourself you are! Your pious confession of sin *makes* you a sinner! To announce your moral bankruptcy is to create it! To "admit" you are a miserable worm before a holy God is to impute unrighteousness to yourself by faith -- surely a perverse twisting of the Reformation gospel!

When you pray for the Kingdom of God to come, where do you suppose it is going to come? Outward from *within*! For it is already *there* like a planted grain of mustard seed that is able to sprout into a tree so vast that all the birds of the heavens may come and nest in its branches.

Jesus came preaching the kingdom of God and explaining it with parables of seeds growing secretly. The lesson? The harvest is ripe! It is time to put in the sickle!

The Book of Revelation envisions a glorious consummation when religion shall be no more! Because in that day the separation between God and humanity will be overcome, as it already has in Christ. There simply is no Temple in the New Jerusalem, because the dwelling of God is henceforth with men and women! So says the text.

In the Bible "Kingdom" is pretty much equivalent to "country." They were all ruled by kings. But I suggest that the phrase "Kingdom of God within you" points beyond the limitations of the word "Kingdom." For there is no more any difference between ruler and ruled!

Marx, a follower of Feuerbach, retained some of the vision of the Bible. He saw that if the Golden Age should ever come, the state would wither away. There would be no need for it. And Jesus Christ has brought that consummation, at least in the kingdom of the soul: there is no servile obedience where the king and his subjects are one. The divine king has doffed his crown, for there is no more ruling to be done. Once more he walks with you in the evening cool of the garden pathways *within*.

What will this mean? I can concretize it for you and for myself, if you wish. When you pray the Lord's Prayer and you get to the part where you ask, "Thy Kingdom come," why don't you visualize it coming to fruition from within, from the only place, in the nature of the case, it *could* come from?

When you receive communion, why don't you experience it as taking the Kingdom of God from out there and bringing it in here?

When you have a moral decision to make, grow up enough to realize that your responsibility is not done when you simply recall which rule you have to obey. Your responsibility is to look at the situation and creatively engage it. You are no one's flunky or slave. *You* are the king! Do what Solomon did: decide for *yourself* what is right!

When you worship and are rapt in wonder, let yourself pause to wonder in astonishment at the divine glory that is within you, that you did not make, and hence which you cannot be absurdly conceited over, but which is simply and gloriously *there*.

Just how "within" you is the kingdom of God? I remember

Preaching Deconstruction

reading somewhere in Panikkar that when we say that God is within us, we do not really mean it. We really think God is like a pill that we have swallowed, a metal plate surgically implanted, a bullet fired into us. In other words: a foreign body that is now on the other side of the skin from where it used to be, but which is still external in its alienness. But to say God is within you must mean that he is truly within you, as your DNA is within you! It has penetrated so deeply that it simply *is* you.

The Kingdom of God is not coming with signs to be observed, nor will they say "Lo, here!" or "There!" for the Kingdom of God is within you! It is behind the eye that sees!

Robert M. Price

The Holiness of Desolation

Old Testament Reading:
Lamentations 2:1-10

*How the Lord in his anger
has set the daughter of Zion under a cloud!
He has cast down from heaven to earth
   the splendor of Israel;
he has not remembered his footstool
   in the day of his anger.
      The Lord has destroyed without mercy
   all the habitations of Jacob;
in his wrath he has broken down
   the strongholds of the daughter of Judah;
he has brought down to the ground in dishonor
   the kingdom and its rulers.
      He has cut down in fierce anger
   all the might of Israel;
he has withdrawn from them his right hand
   in the face of the enemy;
he has burned like a flaming fire in Jacob,
   consuming all around.
      He has bent his bow like an enemy,
   with his right hand set like a foe;*

Preaching Deconstruction

and he has slain all the pride of our eyes
    in the tent of the daughter of Zion;
he has poured out his fury like fire.
        The Lord has become like an enemy,
    he has destroyed Israel;
he has destroyed all its palaces,
    laid in ruins its strongholds;
and he has multiplied in the daughter of Judah
    mourning and lamentation.
        He has broken down his booth like that of a garden,
    laid in ruins the place of his appointed feasts;
the Lord has brought to an end in Zion
    appointed feast and sabbath,
and in his fierce indignation has spurned
    king and priest.
        The Lord has scorned his altar,
    disowned his sanctuary;
he has delivered into the hand of the enemy
    the walls of her palaces;
a clamor was raised in the house of the Lord
    as on the day of an appointed feast.
        The Lord determined to lay in ruins
    the wall of the daughter of Zion;
he marked it off by the line;
    he restrained not his hand from destroying;
he caused rampart and wall to lament,
    they languish together.
        Her gates have sunk into the ground;
    he has ruined and broken her bars;
her king and princes are among the nations;
    the law is no more,

and her prophets obtain
  no vision from the Lord.
    The elders of the daughter of Zion
  sit on the ground in silence;
they have cast dust on their heads
  and put on sackcloth;
the maidens of Jerusalem
  have bowed their heads to the ground.

New Testament Reading:
2 Corinthians 4:8-11

We are afflicted in every way, but not crushed; perplexed, but not driven to despair; persecuted, but not forsaken; struck down, but not destroyed; always carrying in the body the death of Jesus, so that the life of Jesus may also be manifested in our bodies. For while we live we are always being given up to death for Jesus' sake, so that the life of Jesus may be manifested in our mortal flesh.

TEXT:

There are holy places in the world, and I have been to some of them. Places where the presence of something sacred can be felt like an invisible meteorology. Always these places are quiet, and often they are in ruins. The ones that are not already at some stage of dilapidation nonetheless display the signs and symptoms, the promise of coming decay. We feel a sense of divinity in ruined places, abandoned places -- shattered temples on mountaintops, crumbling catacombs, islands where a stone idol stands almost faceless. We never have such feelings in cities or even in natural settings, where the flora and fauna are overly evident. This is why so much is

Preaching Deconstruction

atoned for in wintertime, when a numinous death descends on those chosen lands of our globe. Indeed, winter is not so much the holiest time as it is the holiest place, the visible locus of the divine.
  - *Thomas Ligotti, "Mad Night of Atonement"*

Desolation, it seems, is pregnant with a peculiar holiness. That is the point in the passage I have just read from Thomas Ligotti, and I think it serves as a key to unlock some important biblical images. Indeed it provides the basis for a profound spirituality. And the holiness of desolation may just be the only and best way we can deal with the deadly winters of our lives.

Our Old Testament reading was from the Book of Lamentations. This is a collection of five depressing dirges, all occasioned by the leveling of Jerusalem by the Babylonians and Edomites in 587 BC. In later years we know the laments were sung or recited ritually on the anniversary of the destruction -- which date was also thought to be the future birth date of the Messiah. My guess is that these terrible songs were written precisely to be sung as part of the worship conducted in the very ruins of the Temple by the forlorn Jews left in the land after the Babylonians had deported the aristocracy and the priesthood.

We have this mistaken Sunday School idea that all Jews left the Holy Land during the exile, but in fact it was only the upper crust, whose account of the events we read:

to themselves they were all that mattered, so the way they told it, the land was emptied of Jews pure and simple. But in fact most remained, and they continued to worship at the ruins of Solomon's Temple, magnificent even, or perhaps rather magnificent *especially*, in its ruination. So the Lamentations served as a kind of liturgy of shadows in the ruins of the Temple. O worship the Lord in the desolation of holiness!

I believe that Ligotti is right, or at least I have felt what he has his character say we feel. There *is* a paradoxical holiness in ruination. And I would like for the next few moments to attempt to explain why this should be. A phenomenology of the spirituality of decadence, if you will permit me.

As Mircea Eliade has shown, in one of those academic works that foster religious experience by clarifying its nature, *The Sacred and the Profane*, human beings of all times and climes have not so much cherished abstract definitions of the sacred, as they have implicitly or explicitly pictured the sacred. And this in two ways.

First there is *sacred time*: it seems to us that holiness is resident in the remote past, and that it comes into the present from there. The divine visited the world "once upon a time." That ancient time, whether the time of creation or of the Exodus or of Calvary, is laden with all the glowing magic of mythology.

The holiness of the present lies in our partaking of that sacred past by means of the ritual time-travel of scripture readings, communion suppers, baptisms into the death and resurrection of the Savior thousands of years ago.

Preaching Deconstruction

Today becomes holy by harking back to those holy yesterdays.

Second there is *sacred space*: it seems to us that some places are holy places and others are not because some are closer to or more open to a hidden realm of divinity somewhere above us. The holy place is where the spheres of the upper sacred world and the lower secular world meet.

As when Jacob sleeps at Bethel and dreams that night of having stumbled on the very gate of Heaven. When he awakes he ordains the place a shrine, a zone of holiness, and calls it Bethel, House of God. In later years a mighty temple was built there by King Jeroboam. Pilgrims journeyed there as they do to any shrine, because they think they stand a better chance at gaining an audience with God there.

Ultimately the two categories of sacred space and sacred time merge together: a holy place turns out to qualify as holy because the holy appeared there first at some remote *time*.

Now why the aura of holiness that surrounds a ruined building? And it may be a ruined cathedral or temple -- or it may be an old warehouse whose shattered window panes glow in the moonlight of a quiet night.

It is because the ruins *protrude from the past*. They are fragments of walls that must have continued here, girders that must have reached up there, stained glass shards that must have composed a picture we can half imagine.

They *suggest* what they do not show. Thus they are more potent in their presentation of the holy than they could ever have been when they were intact.

The divine, the sacred, cannot simply be shown, or it

would become an idol. And the worst part of an idol is that it is anticlimactic, disappointing! Surely the Holy must be more than that! Religious effigies do their proper work when we remember that they are mere pointers to the divine, suggesters of the holy. They point the soul to an inconceivable wonder and let us get lost in the contemplation of what we cannot imagine.

And the ruins of desolation are far more effective symbols precisely because of their brokenness. A stairway to heaven that falls away, like the ruins of the Tower of Babel. A mute witness to the holiness it can never reach.

Ruins suggest sacred time because from their broken battlements the eye can trace out the past shape of the complete structure, or it inevitably tries to. The very brokenness draws attention to the building's implied past far more drastically than the complete building itself would.

It is as if the vanished parts of the structure were still present but hidden by a curtain of invisibility. All that protrudes before the seeing eye is the fragments of stone and twisted metal.

Indeed the past of the ruin is more powerfully evident in the ruin than is its present! The vanished past is totally *conspicuous by its absence* in the ruins of the present! And that mysterious past, left unseen to the eye and lending an invisible meaning to the ruins of the present, is redolent of the sacred past. And the same is true of sacred space. It is as if the upper portions of the ruined structure have been engulfed by the descending clouds of the holy heaven, as when the disciples on the Mount of Transfiguration saw, eyes widening, Moses, Elijah, and their Lord swallowed by the falling cloud of the Shekinah glory.

What one can no longer see of the ruined temple makes one think of what one cannot see of the heavenly world. A temple beautiful in its intact glory tempts and invites you to mistake it for the heavenly world. Such is the danger of idolatry: the self-exaltation of the works of the hands of man.

Yet even so, one might perhaps have grown to take the splendor of Solomon's Temple for granted if one had seen it three times a year for many years. How could the resident priests have helped taking it for granted?

But those who gathered at the site of the Temple's ruins after 587 BC? They saw the invisible holiness far more clearly than they ever did when distracted by all of Solomon's golden cherubs and pomegranates!

The holiness of desolation is a prime example of what Derrida calls the doctrine of the trace. That is, a thing, a word, an idea, is given its meaning precisely by the opposite that it does *not* mean. The two are like complementary and therefore opposite pieces of a jigsaw puzzle. Each word, to be what it is, must bear the imprint, the outline, the track, the trace of its opposite. Each term points to its opposite.

Even so, the very *desolation* of divine glory is the strongest *symbol* of divine glory! If such is not yet clear from the example of the Temple of Solomon whose desolation occasioned the holy hymns of the Book of Lamentations, let me move to the New Testament.

In Mark's gospel, when is the first time that one of Jesus' contemporaries recognizes him as the Son of God and says so? Is it after a feeding miracle or a walking on the water? No, Mark says these things produced only dumbfoundment and confusion, even fear.

The first time someone is moved to proclaim, "Truly, this was the Son of God" is when the centurion sees him die *on the cross*!

As Paul says, Christ's divine power is made perfect in *weakness*. Because human weakness, destitution, bereftitude, is the ruin that bespeaks and points to its conspicuously invisible opposite: the power of God!

What does Paul say in the New Testament reading for this morning? His own infirmity serves as the potent trace of the mighty power of Christ. The miserable and utter absence of any power of his own clears the field for the appearance of the holiness of God. It is no longer obscured by the shiny baubles of human ability.

When the illusion of human self-sufficiency is gone, and nothing is seen but the ruins of weakness, then is the time when the power of Christ becomes conspicuous by its absence. It is like anti-matter, if you know your physics. A positron appears for a split instant and then decays, leaving behind it a *charged hole* where it was! When human strength decays after a brief moment of visibility, it leaves behind it a void that radiates the power of God.

If you are in a frozen tundra of darkness and desolation, I charge you: do not imagine that God has abandoned you! The sunny days of religious feelings and spiritual ecstasies were a shiny temple, a fancy idol. Now you find yourself in the ruins, where true holiness may be felt in the depth of the soul's night or the body's pain. It is on the cross that you are God's son or daughter!

Preaching Deconstruction

Enter into the mystery of the terrible spirituality of the Lamentations. Cry out to him in your forsakenness. It may be some comfort to know that in so doing you are closer to him than you have ever been. His invisible power and holiness shine the more brightly from your darkness.

This is no Brer Rabbit trick, whereby you may turn mourning into rejoicing by perversely rejoicing over your mourning. Who is telling you to rejoice? I am simply telling you to know where you are! You sit like Job in the wreckage of a temple that once obscured God. It does so no more. You sit in holiness.

Look past the visible and trace out the shadows of the invisible. It is there that you will find the meaning of your sufferings, the secret holiness of desolation.

Robert M. Price

The Fracture in Scripture

Old Testament Lesson:

Jeremiah 8:8-9
How can you say, 'We are wise, and the law of the Lord is with us'? But, behold, the false pen of the scribes has made it into a lie. The wise men shall be put to shame, they shall be dismayed and taken; lo, they have rejected the word of the Lord, and what wisdom is in them?

Isaiah 29:13
And the Lord said: "[T]his people draw near with their mouth and honor me with their lips, while their hearts are far from me, and their fear of me is a commandment of men learned by rote.

New Testament Lesson

Revelation 22:18-19
I warn everyone who hears the words of the prophecy of this book: if any one adds to them, God will add to him the plagues described in this book, and if any one takes away

from the words of the book of this prophecy, God will take away his share in the tree of life and in the holy city, which are described in this book.

Koran Lesson:
Surah 17:74
And if We had not made thee wholly firm thou mightest almost have inclined unto them a little.

Surah 2:106
Such of Our revelations as We abrogate or cause to be forgotten, we bring (in place) one better or the like thereof. Knowest thou not that Allah is able to do all things?

TEXT:
Revelation 10:1-4
Then I saw another mighty angel coming down from heaven, wrapped in a cloud, with a rainbow over his head, and his face was like the sun, and his legs like pillars of fire. He had a little scroll open in his hand. And he set his right foot on the sea, and his left foot on the land, and called out with a loud voice, like a lion roaring; when he called out, the seven thunders sounded. And when the seven thunders had sounded, I was about to write, but I heard a voice from heaven saying, "Seal up what the seven thunders have said, and do not write it down."

Mark 7:1-8
Now when the Pharisees gathered together to him, with

Robert M. Price

some of the scribes, who had come from Jerusalem, they saw that some of his disciples ate with hands defiled, that is, unwashed. (For the Pharisees, and all the Jews, do not eat unless they wash their hands, observing the tradition of the elders; and when they come from the market place, they do not eat unless they purify themselves; and there are many other traditions which they observe, the washing of cups and pots and vessels of bronze.) And the Pharisees and the scribes asked him, "Why do your disciples not live according to the tradition of the elders, but eat with hands defiled?" And he said to them, "Well did Isaiah prophesy of you hypocrites, as it is written, 'This people honors me with their lips, but their heart is far from me; in vain do they worship me, teaching as doctrines the precepts of men.' You leave the commandment of God, and hold fast the tradition of men."

In recent days you may have heard the news that Oxford University Press published an "Inclusive Language New Testament." You can imagine the reactions this thing is generating. And you can probably predict mine too. I thought it might be worth a sermon, both for its own sake and for that of certain larger issues it raises.

I saw a CNN report in which the reporter asked an editor from Oxford University Press if this were not simply a Politically Correct Bible, a euphemizing of the Bible to fit the newspeak of the times. The editor of course denied that it

Preaching Deconstruction

was just PC. Oh no, she protested, the differences just result from a more accurate translation. This gave me a sense of *deja vu*. And in a moment I realized it was because she was simply doing what all professional spin doctors for the Bible do. They lie like hell. She was just lying. There is no way these new translations have a thing to do with the underlying text.

There is a special irony here; in fact there is a whole mirror image series of ironies, each playing off the other. The first has to do with the supposed authority of the Bible, alias the Word of God. Why did God reveal the Bible, as the Bible's spin doctors like to claim? It was because we miserable humans couldn't be trusted to think for ourselves, to come up with the right answers. So God supplied the instruction manual. Thus the Bible has a unique kind of authority. It says it. You do it. It says it. You believe it.

But what has happened in the case of the Inclusive Language Bible? In this Bible we plainly have human beings altering, emending, doctoring the inspired text because they seem to know better. Better than God? Oxford University Press is sending the Word of God to charm school, or really, I guess, to obedience school. When it is they who ought to be obeying the Word of God. Or at least that's the way it's supposed to be, right?

Only it's never been that way. This PC Bible, the Newspeak Testament, is only an overt case of what is usually covert. Namely, the fact that Bible believers have always used the text as a ventriloquist dummy. Just as Ray Bradbury in *Fahrenheit 451* has Jesus pushing a brand of toothpaste on TV in the future, preachers speak their own opinions in the echo chamber of the Bible so as to make their own beliefs pass for the word of god. Biblical authority is a complete fiction and it always has been. What authority the Bible may possess comes from its wisdom, where it *is* wise.

Now, if the Newspeak Testament defies and exposes the old priestcraft ploy of biblical authority, it may be that it is not so unbiblical in another, more genuine way, after all. Dewey M. Beegle in his book *The Inspiration of Scripture* showed how the traditional dictation model of inspiration was ruled out by the fact that all the biblical books are compilations of traditions that have been reshaped, retold, reinterpreted many times over both before and after being written down. If there is any inspiration, it would have to be located somewhere in that long, apparently fortuitous evolutionary process.

Years later Paul J. Achtemaier took up where Beegle left off. He said that since the biblical text grew in such a gradual and piecemeal fashion, then a responsible, biblical use of the Bible today would mean treating it as the Bible writers themselves treated as much of the Bible as was already available to them. And what did they do with it? They radically reinterpreted it. And this they did even when they had the same frozen model of biblical authority fundamentalists have today. Let me give you a couple of examples.

Gerry read the Book of Revelation's warning to readers not to go editing and rewriting the text. It tells you not to do precisely what Matthew and Luke did to Mark, what Chronicles did to Samuel and Kings. The author wants to safeguard the integrity of his text, and he knows that's not

Preaching Deconstruction

easy. In fact it seems that he himself, or maybe some early scribe, has already disobeyed the warning! *Some*one after all has deleted the mysterious revelation of the seven thunders.

Or the text from Mark 7. I find it deliciously ironic that in it Jesus condemns the scribes for tampering with God's word so as to make room for their own traditions. The irony is double. In the first place, the quote from Isaiah is not from the Hebrew original, but from the Greek Septuagint, and the translation is quite a bit different from the original. So the very scripture citation aimed against tinkering with the scripture is itself a tinkered scripture!

And not only that: to have Jesus saying this to Palestinian Jewish scribes is out of the question, since he would never quote the Greek text! Even the Jewish washing customs Mark refers to did not exist in Palestine! So someone has concocted the story, claiming the divine authority of Jesus for his own opinion! In short, exactly what it condemns the scribes for doing! As Deconstructionists say, the text is self-subverting.

Is the Newspeak Testament really doing anything different? No, I think we have to admit that it is simply continuing the old biblical process of rejuvenating the tradition by changing it, reinterpreting--even rewriting it. Fine. Good for them.

But even here there is an irony, and more of a tragic one. The main tendency of the Newspeak Testament is to make it look like the Bible is not a male-centered, male-biased document. But it is. The Bible is getting a face lift. Again, I admit the goal is to rehabilitate scripture so it can still be a scripture at all. But even if that is what you're doing, think again. The changes in the Bible that we find here are so superficial as to be comical. Because, I submit, the problems go much, much deeper than calling God Father and not Mother.

Mary Daly once said that for someone to seek equality for women in the Catholic Church is like seeking equality for blacks in the Ku Klux Klan! Huston Smith changed his famous book "The Religions of Man" to "The World's Religions." Why? Of course, to eliminate the sexism. Hey, Huston, I've got news for you: why don't you wait to change the title till the religions themselves have changed? That's what they are, all right: the religions of Man. Women are strictly second class citizens.

And in the case of the biblical religions, I think this stems from the pervasive "phallogocentrism" of biblical monotheism. The very idea that the Truth must be One and must be Ultimate and unchallenged seems to stem from the instinct of the bull ape to rule the roost, to play King of the Hill, to combat one's competitors so as to have all the females for oneself.

The Christian preoccupation with True doctrine, with Christ being "of one substance with the Father," comes from paternity anxiety. When asked what each would do should they find out after a couple of months that their baby had been switched with another in the maternity ward, most women say they'd keep the baby they'd bonded with. Most men say they want their own offspring, their own genetic extension. They want the one who is *homoousias* with themselves. Thus the Nicene Creed.

When God is a male, a Father, and the Logos through

Preaching Deconstruction

which the whole world was made is a male, a Son, then you are saying the whole of reality must be understood from a male perspective. I don't see how you're going to correct this all-determining bias in the Bible with the silly etiquette-editing of the Inclusive Language New Testament. What you will need is a largely new Bible. Or maybe no Bible at all, since even the authority trip itself is male chauvinism.

But here's the issue that interests me. Let me go back to the idea of the danger, indeed the inevitability, of the text of the Bible eventually being changed, rewritten, corrupted. This says something very important about textuality in general.

In his book *Limited, Inc.*, Jacques Derrida shows how all language contains a hidden fault-line, a fracture undermining the existence of any fixed or definitive meaning. He uses the image of a postcard. When you send someone a note on a postcard, it is open to all eyes that meet it in transit. Once it gets to the intended recipient, he or she probably will know exactly what your words mean. But no one else will. Others may miss certain in-jokes, pet names, tacit assumptions. Imagine for a moment a postal worker sorting the mail and happening to notice what you wrote on a card. It intrigues and puzzles him. Out of context it may sound sinister, suspicious, salacious. It is the stuff sitcoms are made of.

Can you imagine that postal worker copying down your return address, calling up directory assistance, getting your number, and calling to ask what you really meant? That's the only way he could possibly arrive at the author's meaning. But this is never going to happen. So if he reads the card, that's the text, the beginning and the end of it, right there. It's never going to mean any more than that unaided text is going to tell you by itself.

So the text itself cannot be said to communicate a definitive message. If you know the author and can surmise what the author meant to tell you, the postcard has become something like a smoke signal yielding a message to you alone. But otherwise, it's just a peculiar puff of smoke. An enigma more than a message.

This built-in possibility of a text's being eavesdropped on, listened in on, is a potential included in the text *as* a text. And that potential is actualized in every reading. Even the intended recipient may read the card a second time some days later and come to see implications he did not see at first. As on *M*A*S*H* when Henry rejoices over a letter from his wife telling him she understands if he winds up having sex with other women over in Korea. Only later does he realize what she is really telling him is that she is having an affair with the neighborhood dentist.

The structural possibility of being misunderstood, understood in many ways, means that language does not lend itself to the conveying of a definitive meaning. It is not so precise an instrument as that.

Well, I think that in the same way we can see a fracture in scripture, a built-in possibility of corruptibility that makes the whole notion of a pure text impossible and absurd. The text, any text, is made of certain elements and not others, but these elements function as a kind of DNA, a fund of genetic potential which, though unique, can be combined and recombined, can mutate into a limitless variety of new forms. That, in fact, is what it means for a text to be a living word, not a dead letter. The text is not written in stone, Moses to the contrary, but is malleable.

The Inclusive Language Bible is an example of this evolutionary mutation. So is *The Last Temptation of Christ* And so is *Jesus Christ Superstar*.

We have really only returned in a roundabout way to the point made by Beegle and Achtemaier: the Bible cannot be either inspired or authoritative as a frozen, definitive text. Because no text is such a text. What usefulness the biblical text has is as a flowing stream of new and renewed insights, of new theological and exegetical possibilities. Of new light breaking forth. And, as Heraclitus said, you can't step into the same river twice. It will have changed already.

Let me end with what I believe is a perfect theological symbol for the fracture in scripture both as an inevitable condition of textuality and as a hope for theological and religious renewal as scriptures are read in new ways.

In one of his books on the Jewish Kabbalah, Gershom Scholem tells of the theological dilemma of the Kabbalistic mystics. They believed that the provisions of the Torah, being mostly prohibitions, were specific to this fallen age of sin. In the coming age of Redemption, sin would be eradicated. Thus the old commandments would no longer be of any use. And yet it was blasphemy even to suggest that the Word of God might become superfluous--and equally sacrilegious to say that it might change to meet the needs of the new age. How can the eternal Word of God change, even for the better? It could not.

So their solution was that it would not change. That

is, the sacred text of the Torah would not change. But its aspect would change. Its appearance would change. It would wear a new and benevolent face in the Messianic age. What would make the difference? The secret presence, hitherto unguessed, of a hidden signifier, an invisible letter running through the whole extent of the text. If you could see that letter, all would read differently, as when paleographers expose an old scroll to infrared light and letters they could not read before, because the ancient ink had worn away, suddenly leap into visibility. What had for thousands of years read one way as a commandment against sin, would for the first time be revealed as saying something else, something positive pertaining to the great age of Redemption.

There was a hidden but integral fold at the heart of the text which made it impossible for the text to mean one definite thing for all time. And so it is with every text, with textuality in general, and thus with the text of the Bible. It is, as the Writer to the Hebrews says (at least in the text as we now read it!), alive and powerful. It is powerful only insofar as it is alive, and it lives only if it changes.

Preaching Deconstruction

Mute Oracles

Old Testament Reading:

Daniel 5:1-9
King Belshazzar made a great feast for a thousand of his lords, and drank wine in front of the thousand. Belshazzar, when he tasted the wine, commanded that the vessels of gold and of silver which Nebuchadnezzar his father had taken out of the temple in Jerusalem be brought, that the king and his lords, his wives, and his concubines might drink from them. Then they brought in the golden and silver vessels which had been taken out of the temple, the house of God in Jerusalem; and the king and his lords, his wives, and his concubines drank from them. They drank wine, and praised the gods of gold and silver, bronze, iron, wood, and stone. Immediately the fingers of a man's hand appeared and wrote on the plaster of the wall of the king's palace, opposite the lampstand; and the king saw the hand as it wrote. Then the king's color changed, and his thoughts alarmed him; his limbs gave way, and his knees knocked together. The king cried aloud to bring in the enchanters, the Chaldeans, and the astrologers. The king said to the wise men of Babylon, "Whoever reads this writing, and

shows me its interpretation, shall be clothed with purple, and have a chain of gold about his neck, and shall be the third ruler in the kingdom." Then all the king's wise men came in, but they could not read the writing or make known to the king the interpretation. Then King Belshazzar was greatly alarmed, and his color changed; and his lords were perplexed.

New Testament Reading:

1 Corinthians 13:8 - 14:25
Love never ends; as for prophecies, they will pass away; as for tongues, they will cease; as for knowledge, it will pass away. For our knowledge is imperfect and our prophecy is imperfect; but when the perfect comes, the imperfect will pass away. When I was a child, I spoke like a child, I thought like a child, I reasoned like a child; when I became a man, I gave up childish ways. For now we see in a mirror dimly, but then face to face. Now I know in part; then I shall understand fully, even as I have been fully understood. So faith, hope, love abide, these three; but the greatest of these is love.

Make love your aim, and earnestly desire the spiritual gifts, especially that you may prophesy. For one who speaks in a tongue speaks not to men but to God; for no one understands him, but he utters mysteries in the Spirit. On the other hand, he who prophesies speaks to men for their upbuilding and encouragement and consolation. He who speaks in a tongue edifies himself, but he who prophesies edifies the church. Now I want you all to speak in tongues, but even more to prophesy. He who prophesies is greater than he who speaks in tongues, unless someone interprets, so that the church may be edified.

Now, brethren, if I come to you speaking in tongues,

Preaching Deconstruction

how shall I benefit you unless I bring you some revelation or knowledge or prophecy or teaching? If even lifeless instruments, such as the flute or the harp, do not give distinct notes, how will anyone know what is played? And if the bugle gives an indistinct sound, who will get ready for battle? So with yourselves; if you in a tongue utter speech that is not intelligible, how will anyone know what is said? For you will be speaking into the air. There are doubtless many different languages in the world, and none is without meaning; but if I do not know the meaning of the language, I shall be a foreigner to the speaker and the speaker a foreigner to me. So with yourselves; since you are eager for manifestations of the Spirit, strive to excel in building up the church.

Therefore, he who speaks in a tongue should pray for the power to interpret. For if I pray in a tongue, my spirit prays but my mind is unfruitful. What am I to do? I will pray with the spirit and I will pray with the mind also; I will sing with the spirit and I will sing with the mind also. Otherwise, if you bless with the spirit, how can anyone in the position of an outsider say the "Amen" to your thanksgiving when he does not know what you are saying? For you may give thanks well enough, but the other man is not edified. I thank God that I speak in tongues more than you all; nevertheless, in church I would rather speak five words with my mind, in order to instruct others, than ten thousand words in a tongue.

Brethren, do not be children in your thinking; be babes in evil, but in thinking be mature. In the law it is written, "By men of strange tongues and by the lips of foreigners will I speak to this people, and even then they will not listen to me, says the Lord." Thus, tongues are a sign not for believers but for unbelievers, while prophecy is not for unbelievers but for believers. If, therefore, the whole church assembles and all speak in tongues, and outsiders or unbelievers enter, will they not say that you are mad? But if all prophesy, and an unbeliever or outsider enters, he is convicted by all, he is called to account by all, the secrets of his heart are disclosed; and so, falling on his face, he will worship God and declare that God is really among you.

TEXT:

Acts 2:1-13

When the day of Pentecost had come, they were all together in one place. And suddenly a sound came from heaven like the rush of a mighty wind, and it filled all the house where they were sitting. And there appeared to them tongues as of fire, distributed and resting on each one of them. And they were all filled with the Holy Spirit and began to speak in other tongues, as the Spirit gave them utterance.

Now there were dwelling in Jerusalem Jews, devout men from every nation under heaven. And at this sound the multitude came together, and they were bewildered, because each one heard them speaking in his own language. And they were amazed and wondered, saying, "Are not all these who are speaking Galileans? And how is it that we hear, each of us in his own native language? Parthians and Medes and Elamites and residents of Mesopotamia, Judea and Cappadocia, Pontus and Asia, Phrygia and Pamphylia, Egypt and the parts of Libya belonging to Cyrene, and visitors from Rome, both Jews and proselytes, Cretans and Arabians, we hear them telling in our own tongues the mighty works of God." And all were amazed and perplexed, saying to one another, "What does this mean?" But others mocking said, "They are filled with new

Preaching Deconstruction

wine."

Epigrams:

"Those were his words. And then he talked about the voices of the patients under his care. He whispered, and I quote, that 'the wonderful music of those voices spoke the supreme delirium of the planets as they go round and round like bright puppets dancing in the blackness.' In the wandering words of those lunatics, he told me, the ancient mysteries were restored.

"Like all true mysteriarchs," Mr. Locrian went on, "my grandfather desired a knowledge that was unspoken and unspeakable."

Thomas Ligotti, "Dr. Locrian's Asylum"

Surely the most conspicuous feature of the Pentecost account in Acts chapter two, that passage I am making the object of my scrutiny in this series of Pentecost season sermons, is the outburst of the 120 disciples who, under the afflatus of the Holy Ghost, began to speak in tongues.

Some in the crowd heard what they said as a preaching of the gospel in a discrete foreign language, while others heard only what appeared to be drunken gibberish. I will eventually suggest that it may have been these latter who were closest to a true understanding of the divine oracles they heard that day. But first a closer look at what is going on in the story *vis a vis* these strange tongues.

Interpreters have never been able to agree on just what it is that Luke is trying to describe. On the one hand he sets us up with the knowledge that the crowd contains people who speak many different languages from all over the Eastern Mediterranean basin. Why are they mentioned? Apparently so that we may understand that there are witnesses competent to judge whether or not someone is genuinely speaking a foreign language.

And this seems at first like what the apostles are shown doing. Elsewhere in Acts, as in 1 Corinthians, when people are said to be speaking in inspired frenzy, the expression used is "speaking in tongues." But here and here alone we have it stated that the apostles spoke "in *other* tongues," which would naturally be taken to mean foreign languages, not inspired ranting.

In this case the miracle is how these unlettered Galileans would have gained such expertise, and indeed the point is that they gained it directly from the outpouring of the Holy Spirit, as later when the Sanhedrin marvels that Peter and John can be so well spoken when they are mere Galilean bumpkins without an education.

But if what Luke means is that they were granted the gift of speaking foreign languages they had not learned, why all the emphasis on *hearing*? The passage says three times that various people in the crowd *hear* them speaking in the languages familiar to the crowd. It implies the 120 were simply carrying on in ecstatic ravings which were then *interpreted* spontaneously in the ears of each hearer, like the simultaneous translations in the United Nations, and that was the miracle.

This would also make sense of the otherwise strange detail that *some* of the audience hear nothing but gibberish. "They are filled with new wine!" This is pretty much the

Preaching Deconstruction

response Paul expects the Corinthians to get from outsiders if and when they speak in tongues with no intelligible interpretation attached. "Will they not say that you are mad?"

Some interpreters, baffled by the pulling apart of the text in these two directions, suggest that Luke took an earlier story depicting Christians speaking in unintelligible tongues and reinterpreted it as a speaking of real foreign languages-- or perhaps that he took a language-miracle story and confused it with the phenomenon of speaking in tongues. I suspect something like this happened. The confusion, as often in Luke's writings, is a result of a sloppy and hasty job of editing.

But the result is quite interesting for another reason. The text, confused and confusing as it is, becomes what Paul de Man calls an allegory of its own reading. That is, just as the bystanders in the story are amazed and befuddled at the contrary claims being made around them, "What? Speaking Parthian? Elamite? Palmyran? Sounds like gibberish to me!"--just so, the reader is confronted by a text that seems to be ringing with the dissonance of confusion.

Not only can we not account for the fact of the Galileans speaking in tongues, perhaps intelligible, perhaps not; we cannot even tell whether Luke means foreign or angelic languages! Or is Luke himself simply filled with new wine? Or am I?

But amid this din, perhaps a note of important revelation sounds after all. Can it be that the confusion of tongues is not so much an *obscuring* of what is supposed to be a revelation as it is just what we ought to *expect* from a revelation?

I mean that it can be no simple matter for human lips, even should they be inspired, to speak the Word of God. Not even the coal from the altar with which the Seraph touched Isaiah's lips can really help.

Let's approach it this way: the very phrase which is central to so many Christian denominations, "the Word of God," deconstructs spontaneously into a pile of ill-fitting glossolalic syllables. If it is a *word*, it is a member of the linguistic sign-system constructed by the little minds of human beings to navigate in their world. Words are volleyballs tossed back and forth over the net in the game of human communication.

If one of these words goes bouncing off the court, out of use-context, no points are scored, no meaning taken. The words have meaning, they count, only in the matrix of the game, the language game for which they are designed. If I were to say the sentence "It is *not!*" as I just did, with no context, what meaning could it have?

If a word is a *word*, it cannot be a word *of God*, for then it would be a word spoken from outside the meaning matrix. It would be as if somebody tossed a football into the midst of the volleyball game. It couldn't register. It would be a confusing surd element. If it is a meaningful word, then, it must arise from within the human language game.

But if it is *of God*, it cannot be a word, for God can have no need of them. To suppose he does is to ape the childishness of the writer of Genesis One who has God create the darkness and call it "Night," or the Hebrew word for "Night," as if God spoke Hebrew before there were any

Preaching Deconstruction

human beings on earth, much less Hebrews!

The word of God, if such there be, must sound like thunder from one end of heaven to the other. "There is no speech, nor are there words; their voice is not heard; yet their line is gone out through all the earth, and their words to the end of the world" (Psalm 19:3-4).

Should a prophetic ear catch those echoes, like some great radar dish at NASA, what could it do with them? Would there be any hope at all of translating these echoes into human speech? So even the prophet might understand them?

Here is the distinction implied in 1 Corinthians 14: someone might speak the inspired word and not understand it, only rant and rave, only sound like a drunken babbler--- because there could be no human words appropriate. But Paul supposes that someone else present has the Delphic gift of interpretation and could convey the sense of the divine message. But here's where he's wrong.

The New Critics spoke of the "heresy of paraphrase"-- the impossibility of rendering the unique evocations of a poem in any other medium. You would just destroy the whole thing, the delicate dew-bubble of meaning hanging upon nothing that is a poem, if you turned it into prose.

Vladimir Nabokov wrote a little verse on the utter impossibility of adequately translating even plain prose from one language to another.

> **What is translation? On a platter**
> **A poet's pale and glaring head,**
> **A parrot's screech, a monkey's chatter**

And profanation of the dead.

Just as de Man says that any interpretation is a new work altogether, slyly trying to impersonate the work it pretends merely to elucidate, any human word that pretends to be the Word of God has blasphemously usurped the (empty) throne of the Word of God.

Here is how 1 Corinthians itself puts the error I am talking about: "Now we see in a mirror dimly, but then face to face." That is, in our ignorance, we gaze into a poor, uneven mirror, and we make a crucial mistake about what we see there. What is it? I think the mistake is that *we do not realize it is a mirror*. We think we are looking *into a window*. We think we see something beyond ourselves, when it is *our own image* that confronts us.

We hear and repeat what we think is the very Word of God, but in fact it is only our own human word, the only kind of word we can speak, the only kind there can be. It is perhaps a word that our community of faith has taught us, and we revere it, and we imagine that it is divine in origin, not to be questioned, not to be denied, not to be disbelieved.

But to grow to maturity is to recognize that the sound is our own echo, the image is our own reflection. What do we do then?

We do not fall silent. We continue to speak the only words religion can speak, words of myths and divine intrusions. Words and stories of saviors from the heavens.

But never again can these words become the excuse for cultural or religious imperialism, as they did when the Crusaders warred against the Muslims, crying "God wills it!"

Preaching Deconstruction

As when 19th century missionaries gladly rode the coat-tails of the colonial powers to impose Christianity on Africans while their cynical masters seized their lands.

Never again can these words be mighty enough to damn the unbeliever who refuses to say them. For powerful as they are, they are only our words, and not the words of God.

Never again can these words be unquestionable and unchangeable, as if a description of God that makes of him an arbitrary despot and the heavenly model for despots on earth could not be traded in for something better and more humanizing. We created God the tyrant; we can create a different God-image. And we must.

Religious maturing is the realization that there is no Word of God for poor mortals to parrot, that we must take responsibility for our own words, their greatness and their limitations, and that we have no God-given license to use them as weapons against each other.

That is the lesson I draw this morning from the Pentecost scene: it is a scene in which some strive to speak the Word of God and, insofar as they do, it is only verbal salad. It is a scene where others hear something and articulate it in their own words, make it over in their *own* languages, Parthians, Medes, Elamites, Cappadocians, Cretans and Arabians.

Those are our options. We may pretend to speak the Word of God from heaven, but we will become increasingly unintelligible, even to ourselves, or we can speak in our own languages of the mighty works of God.

Robert M. Price

Jesus in a Bottle

Old Testament: Psalm 56:1-8
>   Be gracious to me, O God,
> for men trample upon me;
>   all day long foemen oppress me;
> my enemies trample upon me all day long,
>   for many fight against me proudly.
> When I am afraid,
>   I put my trust in thee.
> In God, whose word I praise,
>   in God I trust without a fear.
>   What can flesh do to me?
>   All day long they seek to injure my cause;
> all their thoughts are against me for evil.
> They band themselves together, they lurk,
>   they watch my steps.
> As they have waited for my life,
>   so recompense them for their crime;
>   in wrath cast down the peoples, O God!
>   Thou hast kept count of my tossings;
> put thou my tears in thy bottle!
> Are they not in thy book?

Preaching Deconstruction

New Testament: Mark 4:10-12
And when he was alone, those who were about him with the twelve asked him concerning the parables. And he said to them, "To you has been given the secret of the kingdom of God, but for those outside everything is in parables; so that they may indeed see but not perceive, and may indeed hear but not understand; lest they should turn again, and be forgiven."

TEXT:

Thomas saying 13 (Lambden translation)
Jesus said to his disciples, "Compare me to someone and tell me whom I am like."
Simon Peter said to him, "You are like a righteous angel."
Matthew said to him, "You are like a wise philosopher."
Thomas said to him, "Master, my mouth is wholly incapable of saying whom you are like."
Jesus said, "I am not your master. Because you have drunk, you have become intoxicated from the bubbling spring which I have measured out."
And he took him and withdrew and told him three things. When Thomas returned to his companions, they asked him, "What did Jesus say to you?"
Thomas said to them, "If I tell you one of the things which he told me, you will pick up stones and throw them at me; a fire will come out of the stones and burn you up."

A couple of weeks ago I noted that I no longer take a Christocentric, or Christ-centered, perspective. I thought it might be worth addressing the issue in more detail this morning. What I want to suggest to you is that *not* to be Christ-centered, to decide to be *non*-Christocentric, does not mean that you have judged the revelation of Jesus Christ to be deficient in some way, outmoded, inadequate.

I admit that being Christ-centered in the way Christianity traditionally has been, is limiting. It limits the menu of spiritual resources open to you. It limits your willingness to recognize a kindred spirit in people who belong to other religions, as long as you insist they enunciate "Jesus" as a password. But that is not what I have in mind this morning.

Rather, I am saying that to make Christ the center, the bull's eye, is, strangely enough, to limit the power of *Christ*. That is not what any lover of the Christ can possibly intend, and yet I think that is the result of Christocentric fixation.

Let me start with a remarkable passage in the Gospel of Mark, our New Testament reading. In it Jesus tells the puzzled disciples that he teaches in parables for the simple reason that he wants to confound his hearers, to render their eyes and ears useless. "Hey! What's wrong? I've got eyes, but for some reason I don't seem to be seeing! I have ears, but I don't seem to be hearing! What gives?"

Commentators don't want Jesus to have said this. A.M. Hunter, Joachim Jeremias, and other notable exegetes cannot believe their *own* eyes and ears when they come to this saying! Surely, they reason, Jesus must have wanted to communicate his truths to the dull-witted by means of home-spun analogies. He must have wanted to make things *easier* for them, not *harder*, mustn't he?

So these interpreters try to manipulate the underlying

Preaching Deconstruction

Greek or Aramaic words in such a way as to make Jesus say he uses parables *for the sake* of his hearers' hard hearts. He wants to communicate the truth by using creative teaching methods. A matter of educational psychology. Jesus the Ed.D. Yes, it would sure make more sense that way, or at least it would seem more sensible *to us*.

But I think it is contemporary Structuralist and Deconstructive critics who have finally spotted what Jesus may have been up to.

De Man, Barthes, Culler, and others speak of the process of "naturalization," whereby we try to domesticate a strange-sounding text, to harmonize it with what we already believe about the world. Try to find a familiar category for it. We just cannot leave the Other in its Otherness. We can't believe someone could really intend to say So-&-So. So we do him the favor of giving a more natural-seeming interpretation. We always have the tendency to make a text say something *we might expect* it to say, what it would say if *we* wrote it.

But do you see the danger there? For it to "click" with us, for it to *make sense* to us, we must reduce it to a commonplace. Something that no longer sounds startling and outrageous. Albert Schweitzer once blamed New Testament exegetes for whittling down the bizarre sayings of Jesus to manageable proportions. He said the scholars were like a bomb squad whose business it was to go about carefully disarming shells that hadn't exploded yet. Once they are finished, we can be comfortable with the gospels.

Once naturalized, once domesticated, the sayings of Jesus will pose no threat to our complacency. We can go on pretending we are fine.

We can go on unscathed by the fanatical challenges that the texts, while still ticking, seemed to cast in our teeth. We can go on with our clever theologies.

Not following me? Here's an example: "If thy right eye offend thee, pluck it out and cast it away." Just like Oedipus. Only certainly Jesus cannot have meant *this*! *Can* he? "Do not resist the evil one. If a man smite thee on one cheek, turn the other cheek." The attempts to naturalize this one, to evade its force, are legion. Adam Clayton Powell took it to mean this: "Jesus didn't say what to do *next*, and I say *punch* em!" (I know a man doing a dissertation on Powell's use of scripture. I sure hope he hasn't left out *that* little gem!)

"Anyone who does not give up *all that he has* cannot be my disciple." "When you give a feast, do not invite your friends and relatives, lest they repay you. Instead invite the poor, the lame, the blind, the maimed." "Do not lay up for yourselves treasure on earth." *Well* now, we nervously laugh, Jesus can't have meant these things *literally*... And we get to work whittling.

Jesus has nothing to say to us unless we leave his strange sayings in their strangeness! They cannot approach us as a revelation from without if we immediately accommodate them to tepid common sense.

I say that is why he spoke in unintelligible parables which no one has really unraveled in 1900 years! He *wanted* to puzzle his hearers, to shock, to confuse. To send them away scratching their heads! Because that's the only way we can be opened to the invading Spirit! We are normally on guard, carefully fortified against the approach of the Spirit. We must be thrown off guard before he can drive home the decisive blow.

The Zen masters used the same strategy. They knew no enlightenment was possible so long as the seeker had his head filled up with concepts, expectations, complacent definitions of God and the world that became false images *substituting* for God and the world. So their disciples had to be *disabused* of these clogging illusions, these choking concepts, before the lightning of the Spirit could strike! And so they told riddles with no answers. They fastened spiritual locks that no familiar key might open. Like Jesus, they threw their hearers into confusion, knowing that it is only in the midst of such darkness that the word, "Let there be light!" may be spoken.

So the traditional interpreters of Jesus failed to grasp what he was trying to do. He wasn't trying to make it easy for you to reduce his message to something you could already understand. He was tossing out live grenades to shatter your spiritual complacency, to shake you free of your illusions.

But what was true of Jesus' parables is equally true of Jesus himself. Here is the point of our text from Thomas. Jesus wants to test the disciples' spiritual acuity. So he sets a trap to see if they will fall into it. And the first two do. "Make a comparison and tell whom I am like." It's a straight man's line. And Peter and Matthew fall for it. They parrot what seem to have been interpretations of Jesus widespread in Thomas' day: he is a righteous angel, which is what many Jewish Nazoreans thought. Or he is a wise philosopher, which many of his Cynic and Stoic followers thought, the people who wrote up the Q gospel.

But it is only Thomas, the twin brother of Jesus, figuratively the soul mate and reflection of Jesus, the ideal Christian in other words, who understands that the answers must be wrong since they are answers to the wrong question in the first place. For it is *utterly impossible* to say what Jesus is like. It is impossible to reduce him, to reduce the spiritual dynamism he represents, to a neat formula.

Any concept of Jesus, the Thomas text seems to say, is a misleading oversimplification. And thus in this whole Gospel of some 114 sayings, Jesus is never once called the Christ, the Son of God, the Son of Man, etc.

And this is not only because any one Christ-concept would be reductionistic. It is also because the minute you propose a concept of Jesus and the minute I believe in it, we have erected an idol of Jesus, no different from the dashboard plastic Jesus. We have forsaken the Living One. We have pushed a stopper into the bottle of living waters.

But Thomas stands for any would-be follower of Jesus who has known not to stop up the water. Jesus blesses him, not because he has said the right thing about Jesus--*because there can be no right thing to say about him!*--but rather because he has followed Jesus to the stream of living water and drunk from it himself. That is what you must do. And what is the reaction of the institutional church to this insight? What has it always been? Institutions are based on obedience, conformity, "getting with the program," not rocking the boat. The loyal subject of traditional Christianity's hegemony over the spirit does not think to seek the wells of which Jesus himself drank. He wants only to know *that* Jesus drank. He wants to think that Jesus *alone* ever drank, that he alone *could* ever drink.

And this is why, in our passage, Thomas refuses the request of Peter and Matthew. He declines to throw his pearls before swine because he knows too well what will happen if he does! They will tread them underfoot with accusations of "Blasphemy!" and turn on him and tear him to pieces. Such is the history of religious inquisitions.

I mentioned Albert Schweitzer, a great medical missionary because he was first a great New Testament exegete. He was overtaken by the outlandish commands of Jesus to take up the cross, and so he spent his life in the service of the disease-racked multitudes of Central Africa. Here are two things Schweitzer said of Jesus in his great book *The Quest of the Historical Jesus*. I think they are closely connected.

> *Jesus means something to our world because a mighty spiritual force streams forth from him and flows through our time also. This fact can neither be shaken nor confirmed by any historical discovery. It is the solid foundation of Christianity.*

> *He comes to us as one unknown, without a name, as of old, by the lake-side, he came to those who knew him not. He speaks to us the same word: Follow thou me! and sets us to the tasks which he has to fulfill in our time. He commands. And to those who obey him, whether they be wise or simple, he will reveal himself in the toils, the conflicts, the sufferings which*

they shall pass through in his fellowship, and, as an ineffable mystery, they shall learn in their own experience who he is.

There is a connection, I say. Jesus can unleash a mighty spiritual current that keeps building in force precisely because he refuses to let anyone stop up the flood by erecting some great Hoover Dam with a Christocentric creed written across its surface.

You must be baptized in that stream if you are to take Jesus seriously. I don't mean get the right idea of him. It's not a question of that. Thomas is quite right. Because doctrines are bottle caps, trophies, relics. It is the spiritual force that matters.

You will never construct any coherent ethical or doctrinal theory from Jesus' sayings. That would be another way of domesticating them. Whittling them. The point is to play dodge ball with Jesus, to stand in the lightning storm he has unleashed. Turn the other cheek, invite the poor, give away your possessions. Fast. *Don't* fast. (He says both!) You need to be kept off balance, decentered.

Spirituality can enter only through surprise. We guard against it. So we must be taken off our guard. And Jesus does this by keeping us guessing. Knocking down any house of cards as soon as we build it. This is the only way to remain open to the stream of Jesus: by not freezing it into a glacier of doctrine. Least of all a doctrine about Jesus! A Christology, a definitive definition of Jesus, is a tombstone for Jesus, who is alive in the elusive and baffling teaching attributed to him.

About the Author

Robert M. Price has taught religion, theology, philosophy, world religions, and Bible in colleges, seminaries, and universities. Now most of his teaching is done via his podcasts *The Bible Geek* and *The Human Bible*. He has written numerous books including *Beyond Born Again, Inerrant the Wind, The Widow Traditions in Luke-Acts, Jesus Is Dead, The Incredible Shrinking Son of Man, Deconstructing Jesus, The Christ Myth Theory and its Problems, Secret Scrolls*, and others. He has also served as a campus minister for the United Ministries in Higher Education and as pastor of the First Baptist Church of Montclair, NJ. He holds Ph.D. degrees in both Theology and New Testament. He speaks and writes for atheist and secular humanist groups but also infuriates them by remaining friendly to religion and conservative in his politics. (Are you alienated yet?) He is the subject of the forthcoming documentary *The Gospel According to Price*.

Price is also a big wheel in the world of H.P. Lovecraft scholarship and fandom. He founded *Crypt of Cthulhu* and edited 107 issues of it. He has compiled shelves of Cthulhu Mythos anthologies for Fedogan & Bremer, Chaosium, Inc., Arkham House, and others. His own horror fiction is collected in *Blasphemies and Revelations*. He hosts the podcast *The Lovecraft Geek*.

While serving as a church pastor and working on his New Testament doctorate, Price discovered Deconstruction and felt a new world opening up to him. The present volume collects several of his sermons from that period.

www.ingramcontent.com/pod-product-compliance
Lightning Source LLC
Chambersburg PA
CBHW020005050426
42450CB00005B/316